Corporate Governance
The Indian S——

G000090702

Vasudha Joshi

BOOKS

Delhi • Bangalore • Mumbai • Kolkata • Chennai • Hyderabad

Published by:
Cambridge University Press India Pvt. Ltd.
under the imprint of Foundation Books
Cambridge House
4381/4 Ansari Road
Daryaganj
New Delhi- 110 002

C-22, C-Block, Brigade M.M., K.R. Road, Jayanagar, **Bangalore**- 560 070
Plot No. 80, Service Industries, Shirvane, Sector-1, Nerul, **Navi Mumbai**- 400 706
10, Raja Subodh Mullick Square, 2nd Floor, **Kolkata**- 700 013
21/1 (New No. 49), 1st Floor, Model School Road, Thousand Lights, **Chennai**- 600 006
House No. 3-5-874/6/4, (Near Apollo Hospital), Hyderguda, **Hyderabad**- 500 029

© Cambridge University Press India Pvt. Ltd.
First Edition 2004

ISBN: 978-81-7596-204-0 (Paperback)

Published by Manas Saikia for Cambridge University Press India Pvt. Ltd.

Contents

Part II

Preface

Corporate Governance was a new term a decade ago. Today it is used in common parlance but its meaning is not necessarily understood. In fact, the term is in the danger of passing from an unknown to a cliche without any stages in-between. Company executives have a very narrow idea of corporate governance.

Much of the existing literature on the subject suffers from the same drawback. It has largely taken a narrow, rule book-based approach. Consequently, while a few aspects are flogged repeatedly, there is hardly any attempt to systematically fit various happenings in the theoretical framework. What I have hoped to do in this book is to bring a critical social science perspective to this subject and to relate practice to theory on one hand and Indian developments to those elsewhere, on the other.

The scope of the subject has become wide today. Apart from firm-specific factors, a number of macro-level and institutional variables such as capital market legal system, investors rights and historical evolution of corporate governance system etc. are included in the discourse. Putting all these variables together, coherently, is difficult. I leave it to the readers to judge how far I have succeeded in facing this challenge. The area of corporate ethics has been omitted for its 'behind the doors' nature and lack of hard data.

This work was made possible by a generous research associateship scheme of the UGC. The scheme halved my teaching work and authorities of Ness Wadia College of Commerce, Pune where I teach, put up with a lot of inconvenience to enable me to concentrate on this research. I am grateful to them.

Dr SL Joshi and Dr Capt. CM Chitale, Head Department of Commerce and Management Studies, University of Pune, gave continuous encouragement for this work. Administrative staff of this department and also Finance Department of University of Pune has helped me in innumerable small matters. I take this opportunity to thank them all.

Much of my work was carried out in the pleasant surroundings of the library of National Institute of Bank Management, Pune whose staff members were very helpful. Some tentative feelers I sent out to industrial units, met with positive response and that strengthened my confidence. I am grateful to Mr James Grassom, Dr LC Gupta and Mr AV Rajwade for giving their comments on the early draft of my manuscript. I thank Dr KR Chandratre, Ms Aditi Chirmule

(Kirloskar Oil Engines Ltd.), Mr Satish Sekhri (Kalyani Brakes Ltd.) and Mr Dileep Deshpande (Zensar Technologies Ltd.) for their cooperation.

I thank Mr K Rajeevan of Foundation Books for bringing out the book in a short time.

My parents – PM and Kumudini Joshi – will be relieved to see my long hours of toil take some concrete shape. They have been encouraging throughout. I would have been seriously handicapped without their support. Many more persons have helped me in different ways. I thank them all without naming them.

I hope this book proves useful to students, practitioners and other interested readers. Feedback from readers will be highly appreciated.

1

Corporate Governance: Placing the Issues

Introduction

Corporate Governance was the most important topic of popular as well as academic debate in the 1980s and the 1990s. In the coming years too, interest in this topic is not likely to wane. The interest in corporate governance is primarily due to two factors: curious happenings in the corporate world and the globally mobile capital flows which are highlighting differences in corporate governance systems, in different parts of the world. In the last two decades, many businesses have collapsed. Scandals such as BCCI, Maxwell Communications and Polly Peck appear to be less important today only because Enron, Arthur Andersen, WorldCom and scores of other businesses have plumbed new depths in fraudulent practices. *The Economist* (May, 2002) has started dividing various happenings in this field into two periods – pre-Enron and post-Enron!

Many of these businesses had clean audit reports. The stories doing the rounds since the collapse of Enron include one about the make-believe trading hall, built at a cost of half-a-million dollars to simply create an impression of frenzied activity among investors. Unethical consultancy and other business dealings between companies and their auditors have been found and by hindsight it is realized that the issue of conflict of interest was never seriously addressed in them. Some high profile executive have been put behind bars. Excessive pay package for executives has made shareholders and some big corporations considerably poorer.

In the wake of these murky events, committees are busy making recommendations that will ostensibly correct these wrongs. Takeovers in the capital market have put new managerial teams in office in some big companies. Shareholders are being exhorted to act as serious owners and not just portfolio investors who offload their holdings at the drop of a hat. Institutional investors have started paying heed to this advice. At the same time, employees, consumers, suppliers and small creditors of businesses are lamenting that in the change and controversy created by the above mentioned factors, their interests have been given a short shrift. Many analysts are complaining that excessive importance accorded to shareholder value as a result of this upheaval is undermining long-term sustainability of businesses.

Scandals, frauds, embezzlement of funds and failures are not new to business world. The first documented failure of governance in this world was the South Sea Bubble in the 1700s. It led to some qualitative improvement in business practices and laws in England. Similarly, much of the securities law in the USA was put in place after the capital market collapse of 1929. It would seem that major business lapses and failures lead to changes in governance apparatus of businesses and that this process is continuing without any end in sight. The period from the end of the Second World War till the mid-1970s was a comparatively stable and peaceful period. Pressure for reformation of corporate governance has heightened in the last two decades. This change and constant adaptation to it, impart flexibility and make this system resilient.

The upheaval witnessed since the 1980s, has therefore led to some positive results also. For one thing, there is increased awareness of the issue of corporate governance and its importance. For the first time, a holistic view is being taken of the corporate economy and different models and systems of corporate governance are being compared. In the USA, directors have begun to take their responsibilities more seriously and they have shown willingness to confront chief executives and to remove them from their posts, if necessary. Orientation/training courses for directors, as also courses on ethics and values in business for executives have become popular. There is growing awareness of the importance of shareholder value. Previously, American CEOs would have been hard put to even name their big shareholders. Now they are in close touch with them on an on-going basis. As big institutional investors, pension funds such as Teachers Insurance and Annuity Association-College Retirement Equities Fund (TIAA-CREF) and California Public Employees Retirement System (CalPERS) have become powerful players in corporate governance. All over the world, the press has taken a keen interest in reporting and highlighting major happenings in business world. It has also acquired specialization of a high level in financial and related matters. For instance, *Fortune 500* has taken to publishing an annual list of America's worst boards of directors and furious negotiations are initiated by companies for avoiding to appear in it. Important improvements have been made in legal and other regulations. Different corporate governance systems are converging to some extent due to active capital flows all over the world.

These developments engage our attention and force us to seek means to improve the performance of the corporate economy because there is no getting away from the corporation and its activities. The corporate firm is a prominent player in all markets dealing in goods and services and factors of production i.e. capital and human resources. The ability of the corporation to attract investments, generate profits and create employment has a direct bearing on economic prosperity of the country in which it is located. So the solution lies not in discarding, disregarding the corporate economy but in improving it as best as we can.

Backdrop: change in 'real' factors

Initial discussions of corporate governance tended to concentrate exclusively on the board of directors. Today the scope of the subject has become truly wide. Apart from the working of the board, role of secondary capital market, institutional shareholders proxy contests, leveraged and management buy-outs, role of other stakeholders – particularly employees – and comparison of different corporate governance systems in the world etc. are important aspects of current discussion of corporate governance.

This constantly widening area of theoretical and academic interest is of course backed by and is a response to important shifts in real factors. The oil price shock in 1973 and breakdown of the Bretton Woods foreign exchange rate management system marked a watershed in the role of large business corporations in the West. Prior to 1973, large manufacturing companies such as General Motors, General Electric, AT&T, and IBM dominated US economy which in turn dominated the world economy. These corporations enjoyed stable prospects in product markets and on the basis of their economic clout, they allowed their executives almost unlimited discretion to set their own priorities. And indeed, a variety of objectives other than maximum profits was pursued by them. They made large contributions to research, social and cultural causes and in the tradition of benevolent paternalism, they were sensitive to their social responsibility. By adhering to Fordist principles, managers and workers were given a share in the prosperity of these bodies. This phase of corporate development has been described as *managerial capitalism*.

Economic stability which led to this phase was completely upset by the following developments in the post-1973 period:

- greater competition in product markets, particularly since the entry of Japanese goods
- slowing down of growth
- technological tumult caused by the confluence of information and communication technologies; other industries such as steel, automobiles and pharmaceuticals were temporarily totally eclipsed in this shift
- globalization of the capital market and rapid movements of 'hot money' (for portfolio investment) all over the world
- decline in the economic role of the state
- turbulence in the market for corporate control (i.e. secondary capital market) in the USA.

Heightened activity in terms of mergers, break-ups, buy-outs and takeovers were seen in the 1980s. To defend themselves against takeovers, managers adopted a number of restrictive measures such as poison pills, greenmail (pp 44–45), multiple class shares, staggered boards etc. They also sought greater use of debt and international equity. Stock options were given to employees in the hope that they would support incumbent managements. Stock options to managers turn out to be virtual villains in this saga, according to shareholder-control perspective on corporate governance. (See Chapter 2 and 4 for more details.)

These changes naturally led to profound shifts in the working of corporations. Pressure of competition put a premium on flexibility and steep organizational hierarchies became increasingly flat. Downsizing and re-engineering led to reduced workforce. Employer – employee relations became contingent and non-permanent. With the introduction of foreign equity, pressure for transparency in governance increased. Institutional investors began to bring down the scope for managerial discretion. So managers were forced to concentrate on short-term profits, dividends and stock prices. This can be described as *investor capitalism*. Much of corporate governance literature is devoted to understanding the implications of the shift from managerial to investor capitalism that has been seen in the USA in recent times.

As the capital market became globally integrated in the above period, details of the different corporate governance pattern in Germany and Japan could be studied. The secondary capital market which provides exit option to unhappy investors in the Anglo-American system is not important in this pattern. So it enjoys greater stability. Its defining characteristic is relational investment which provides dedicated capital of banks or other businesses to individual companies. In both Germany and Japan, roughly 70 per cent of outstanding corporate equity is held by other companies – financial and non-financial. Banks and financial institutions are allowed to own equity in both the countries. Keeping arms-length distance between industrial and financial capital to prevent concentration of economic power is, on the other hand, basic to Anglo-American corporate governance system. The main bank of a company in Japan screens loan applications, continuously reviews operational performance and intervenes directly during difficulties. Banks play an important role as creditors in corporate governance in Japan.

German corporations have a two-tier board structure which consists of a managerial and a supervisory board. The latter is sensitive to expectations of other stakeholders, particularly employees who have one-third seats on it. The supervisory board is fairly effective in checking managerial exuberance. The German-Japanese corporate governance system gives effective voice option to majority shareholders and it has also given freedom to management to pursue long-term goals of growth, rising market share, build-up of innovative capacity through research and development etc. Instead of focusing on short-term profits, it looks at long-term sustainability of business and growth. Employee welfare and obligations to local community are more important to German business, while in

Japan, size and market share become principal corporate objectives. According to Porter (1992), this pattern earns higher social returns because it is better able to internalize externalities. Of course, it is not foolproof. It leads to concentration of power, creation of excess capacity, lax investment criteria etc. The recession of 1997 in Japan has eroded the clout of the main bank system. Still, stability, focus on the long-term, a broader, stakeholder-inclusive perspective of corporate mission remain some attractive attributes of this system.

Details of the working of different corporate governance systems and their comparison have brought out many intricacies and consequently, this topic has now become very complex. Also there are new developments taking place every day and it is necessary to relate them to appropriate theoretical constructs, to understand them fully.

Importance of Corporate Governance

Corporate governance is concerned with direction and control of corporate bodies. These activities are far more basic as compared to profitability and performance of companies. They lay the foundation for future progress of business. Corporate governance is the framework that ensures accountability. Once it is in place, firms are free to go about their way in creating shareholder value and registering growth.

In less developed countries, corporate governance is a prerequisite of capital market development. New investors can be encouraged to invest in corporate securities only when there is a credible corporate governance in force. Without it, investors will not come forward to stake their money in companies and private limited companies will not come forward to list their shares on stock exchanges.

It is sometimes argued that corporate governance mechanism is an alternative to competitive markets. The implication is that competition in product and capital markets can make up for deficiencies in corporate governance. This is a wrong notion. Markets may take time to react; they can be deliberately misled and their corrective action may be very drastic. Past evidence shows that efficient, developed markets do not guarantee good governance. It is better to view governance as an assistance to competition: good governance speeds up competitive adaptation and bad governance slows it down. So whether markets are developed or under-developed, corporate governance remains a priority area.

Because of the developments in the last two decades, it is now increasingly found that retail investors, banks, mutual funds and other institutional investors base their investment decisions not only on the future outlook of a company but also its governance. Good governance is becoming a source of competitive advantage among economies for attracting international capital. As mentioned above, it is necessary also to broaden and deepen local capital markets by attracting local investors. It is found that a poor corporate governance system results not only in under-performance in the corporate economy but also in vulnerability of the entire financial system. The growing need to access all types of financial resources and to harness the power of private sector for economic and social progress has brought corporate governance in prominence the world over.

There are different corporate governance systems in the world, each with its plus and minus points and it is not possible to adjudge the best or the ideal one among them. Literature on corporate governance continues to throw up many variables with complex, little understood interrelations. Links between financial, corporate and legal systems are beginning to be unravelled now and dipping a little into this writing, leads to a strong feeling that the more we know about corporate governance, the less we actually know of it. With competitive product and financial markets, with individual or institutional block holders firmly in saddle and with a legal system that gives good protection to investors, corporate governance might become a non-issue. So an impression is created that corporate governance does not matter.

Yet this emerging approach of looking at corporate economy as a whole is highly fruitful. Decision-makers in this economy and also young aspirants must know how the different parts of a corporate governance system fit together. Issues such as scope for managerial opportunism, exploitation of minority shareholders and experiments in new forms of governance need to be focused on again and again to avoid fraud and company failures, to create accountability and to facilitate further progress of corporate economy.

The basic thrust of current corporate governance discussion is on greater accountability of corporate firms but it must be remembered that *autonomy* is equally important in corporate governance. Corporate scandals and frauds have probably forced us to be excessively sensitive to accountability. However, both autonomy and accountability are necessary to corporate governance. With too much importance attached to accountability, it is possible that CEOs and directors will become risk-averse, a box-ticking approach will develop among auditors and executives and businesses will prefer to remain private. These developments will mar future progress of the corporate economy. So both autonomy and accountability must exist together. Autonomy without accountability means the kind of frauds and excesses that have been seen in the last two decades. Accountability without autonomy will only serve to dampen risk-taking, innovative approach to problems of reacting adequately to changing markets, technology and it will bring about a bureaucratic set-up in businesses.

Therefore, depending upon current events, there will be swings of pendulum, sometimes towards accountability and sometimes towards autonomy. However, we need both together.

Some Definitions

Given the variety of perspectives and models of corporate governance (See Chapter 4) it is not surprising that there exist many definitions of corporate governance. Some have a narrow, operational focus and they equate corporate governance with the working of the board of directors for ensuring accountability of senior management. Broad definitions of corporate governance cover the entire network of formal and informal relations in the corporate economy and their consequences for society in general. Some narrow definitions make corporate governance a concern of no one else but the company secretary while the broader ones make it an important public policy issue.

Cadbury Committee (1992) defined corporate governance as the system by which companies are directed and controlled. It is a simple and concise definition that goes to the heart of the matter. It talks about a system (not individual parts), direction (by the board) and control (by shareholders) of businesses.

The World Bank (1999) states that from a corporate perspective, corporate governance is about maximizing value subject to meeting the company's financial, legal and contractual obligations. From a public perspective, corporate governance is about nurturing an enterprise while ensuring accountability in the exercise of power and patronage by firms. The bank states further that the role of public policy is to provide firms with the incentives and discipline to minimize the divergence between private and social returns and to protect the interests of stakeholders.

The above definition rightly talks of *nurturing* businesses while holding them accountable. In deserving cases, autonomy must be provided and similarly the burden of governance rules and regulations must not be so heavy as to throttle the spirit of enterprise. This tightrope walking is essential in governance.

As per **OECD Code on Corporate Governance** (1999), it is a set of relationships between a company's management, its board, its shareholders and other stakeholders. Through these relationships it provides a structure for setting the objectives of the company, the means for attaining them and monitoring performance. Good corporate governance should provide incentives to the board and management to pursue objectives which are in the interests of the company and shareholders and it should also facilitate effective monitoring.

According to **Mary O'Sullivan** (1998) corporate governance is a system comprising social institutions that influence the process of strategic investment in corporates which revolves around three major decisions viz. what types of investments or resource allocations are made, who controls this decision and how are returns from successful investments distributed.

In sharp contrast to the above definitions setting out the big picture, stand some focused definitions which are rooted in the principal-agent model of corporate governance (explained subsequently). Only two of them are reproduced here:

Shleifer, Vishny (1997): Corporate governance deals with the ways in which suppliers of finance to corporations assure themselves of getting a return on their investment.

Oliver Hart (1995): Corporate governance is the sum of processes by which investors attempt to minimize the transaction and agency costs of doing business with a firm.

Principles of Corporate Governance

Because of the deliberations of various groups and committees on corporate governance, a set of principles is available today. Three sets of these principles are set out in the chart below. Out of them, OECD principles are the most comprehensive and widely-known ones. They are explained below.

Table 1.1. *Corporate Governance Principles – A Comparison*

Sl. No.	OECD	APEC (Asia Pacific Economic Cooperation)	Hampel Committee (1998)
1	Rights of shareholders	Establishment of rights and responsibilities of shareholders	—
2	Equitable treatment of all shareholders	Equitable treatment of all shareholders	Shareholders – institutional, shareholder's policy for voting on their shares, dialogue with the company and their views about the company's governance structure
3	Role of stakeholders in corporate governance	Establishment of effective and enforceable accountability standards	—
4	Disclosure and transparency	Timely and accurate disclosure of financial, non-financial information regarding company performance	—
5	Board responsibilities	Establishment of rights and responsibilities of directors and managers	Formation of board of directors and directors' remuneration

OECD principles focus only on those governance problems which arise because of separation between ownership and control of capital.

Right of Shareholders
Corporate governance framework should protect shareholders' rights such as

right to attend and participate in Annual General Meeting (AGM), to elect members of Board of Directors, to receive a share in company profits, to obtain relevant information on the company in a timely, regular basis, to transfer shares etc.

Capital structures and arrangements which enable certain shareholders to obtain control disproportionate to their holding should be disclosed.

Markets for corporate control should be allowed to function in an efficient and transparent manner. Rules about acquisition of corporate control and extraordinary transactions such as mergers and substantial sale of corporate assets should be disclosed. Transactions should occur at transparent prices and under fair conditions. Anti-takeover devices should not be used to shield management from accountability. Institutional shareholders should consider the costs and benefits of exercising their voting rights.

Equitable Treatment of Shareholders

All shareholders including minority and foreign shareholders should get equitable treatment. All shareholders should have the opportunity to obtain effective redress for violation of their rights.

Any change in voting rights should be subject to shareholder vote. Shareholders should not face undue difficulties in exercising their voting rights.

Insider trading and abusive self-dealing should be prohibited.

Directors should avoid situations involving conflict of interest while making decisions. Interested directors should not participate in deliberations leading to certain decisions.

Role of Stakeholders in Corporate Governance

Corporate governance framework should recognize the rights of stakeholders as established by law and encourage active cooperation between the company and stakeholders in creating sustainability of financially sound enterprises. It should permit performance enhancing mechanisms such as employee representation on board of directors, employee stock option plans, profit sharing, creditors' involvement in insolvency proceeding etc. for stakeholders' participation. Where stakeholders participate in corporate governance process, they should have access to relevant information.

Disclosure and Transparency

Corporate governance framework should ensure that timely and accurate disclosure is made on the following points: (Disclosure should not remain limited to these points.)

- financial and operating results
- company objective
- major share ownership and voting rights
- directors, key executives and their remuneration
- significant foreseeable risk factors
- material issues regarding employees and other stakeholders
- governance structures and policies.

Board Responsibilities

Key responsibilities of the board are specified. They include – overseeing the process of disclosure and communication, monitoring effectiveness of governance practices and changing them as necessary.

OECD principles are very comprehensive. Particular note should be made of what they have to say on voting rights of institutional shareholders and obligations of the board to stakeholders. APEC principles reiterate them but give foremost importance to disclosures. Instead of rights of shareholders, they talk of rights and *responsibilities* of shareholders, directors and managers. Establishment of accountability standards is a separate principle according to them.

Part I

2

Major Corporate Governance Systems

Davis Global Advisers Inc. is a consulting firm in the US carrying out research in corporate governance across countries. It prepares a score-card for different countries by comparing their record against the following 10 indicators:

A. Board Structure

1 Code of best practices
2 Non-executive directors
3 Separation between positions of Chairman and CEO
4 Board committees

B. Voting Rights

5 Voting procedure
6 Voting rights
7 Voting issues

C. Disclosure

8 Accounting standards
9 Executive pay disclosure

D. Takeover Defenses

10 Takeover barriers

The firm has compared corporate governance practices in France, Germany, the UK and the USA and has consistently given the highest rank to the UK for her more balanced boards and high level of shareholder rights. British managers also experience the greatest difficulty in erecting takeover defenses which is a point in favour of their corporate governance system. The USA ranks second and France, third. France has recorded the highest score on voting rights. Very powerful CEOs and comparatively fewer investor rights are problems of the USA, according to this study. More details of the firm's assessment of German and Japanese corporate governance systems were not available but their comparison with the above countries would not be easy. The systems differ in important respects.

In the USA, shareholders have a big say in the running of the firms which they own and workers who are weakly organized have little influence. In Germany, on the other hand, workers enjoy much greater influence as compared to shareholders. In Japanese corporate governance system, shareholders have had no role beyond providing capital and company executives enjoy a good deal of autonomy. Michael Porter (1992), has compared the Anglo-American corporate governance system with the German-Japanese system and has shown that capital markets and firms' internal environments differ in important respects in them. Fluid capital, fragmented and transient ownership of capital are found in the USA and the UK and their capital market is transaction-driven. In Germany and Japan, on the other hand, we observe relationship-driven governance with dedicated capital, significant stakes and long-term ownership. Small shareholders are denied 'voice' option and since secondary capital market is not important, they are denied 'exit' option also. Maximum return on investment is the primary corporate objective in the USA, the UK while its place is taken by secure market position and perpetuity in Germany and Japan. Directors exert little influence in the former and there is generally limited flow of information from management to directors and owners. In contrast, in Germany and Japan, block holders or big owners and directors have sizeable influence and information flows extensively among management, directors and majority shareholders.

Different patterns of corporate control which exist in the world, can be summarized in the following manner:

Sl. No.	Type of control	Mechanism of exercising control
1	Management control	Senior executive positions, seats on board of directors
2	Ownership control	Block holders or majority shareholders
3	Financial control	Seats on the board for creditors
4	Control through business group or network	Control over a holding company or apex group the company at the center of a corporate network
5	Political control	Government control, control by workers

Corporate governance systems differ from each other in terms of following important features:

- **Ownership pattern:** concentrated versus dispersed,
- **Objective:** shareholder value versus organizational/employee/other stakeholder welfare and long-term corporate value
- **Decision-making method:** checks and balances versus networks.

There exist other fundamental differences in the above systems. They are summarized in Table 2.2 on the following page. These are important differences and they have far-reaching consequences. More important among them are the differences in corporate control mechanisms as summarized in Table 2.1 below:

Table 2.1. *Importance of different control mechanisms in large non-financial companies*

Sl. No.	Mechanism	Anglo-American governance	German corporate governance	Japanese corporate governance
1	Importance of pay-performance linkage in exeutive compensation	Small	Important in case of owner-managed firms	Small
2	Board independence/ power over management	Little	Greatest	Little formally, more influence informally
3	Monitoring by financial institutions	Little	Some	Substantial
4	Monitoring by nonfinancial companies/ promoters	Little	Substantial	Some
5	Monitoring by individual shareholders	Little	Substantial in case of owner-managed firms	Little
6	Hostile takeovers	Substantial	Virtually non-existent	Virtually non-existent

(Adapted from Stephen Prowse, BIS Economic Paper, No. 41, 1994)

American Corporate Governance System

Brief Historical Background

For over a century from 1850 to 1970, this system has been characterized by organization-control perspective. Since then, there has been a shift towards capital market-control perspective. (These terms are explained in Chapter 4.)

Table 2.2. *Differences in corporate governance*

Sl. No.	Feature	Anglo-American corporate governance	German corporate governance	Japanese corporate governance
1	Objective	Shareholder value	Long-term corporate value	Long-term corporate value
2	Shareholding	Diffused. Institutional investors important block holders currently.	concentrated with banks, promotor families, other corporate firms	concentrated with financial, nonfinancial corporates
3	Governance focus	Capital market	Corporate body	*Keiretsu* or business network
4	Measure of success	Return on financial capital	Return on human capital	Return on social capital
5	Decision-making	Checks and balances between voice and exit options. Outside stakeholders excluded.	Within the network of stakeholders including employees, local community	Within the network which includes business associates and banks as stakeholders
6	Control of corporate firms	Separated from ownership	Linked with ownership	Linked with ownership
7	Orientation	Short-term, driven by stock market prices	Long-term	Long-term
8	Long-term investment in	Physical capital, R & D, human capital	Plant and equipment, employee training	R & D, employee training
9	Capital market: Primary	Liquid	Less important because of close ties with banks	Less important because of close ties with banks
10	Capital market: Secondary	Important, hostile takeovers possible, frequent	Not important, hostile takeovers rare	Not important, hostile takeovers rare
11	Investor commitment	Low	High, important in difficult times	High, important in difficult times

(contd.)

(*Table 2.2 contd.*)

Sl. No.	Feature	Anglo-American corporate governance	German corporate governance	Japanese corporate governance
12	Participant claim ranking	a. Institutionl shareholders b. Individual shareholders c. Business network d. Employees e. Government f. Banks	a. Banks b. Business network c. Employees d. Government e. Individual shareholders, f. Institutionl shareholders	a. Business network b. Main bank c. Government d. Institutionl shareholders e. Individual shareholders f. Employees
13	Composition of Board of Directors	Executive and non-executive directors, former more important till the 1990s	Two-tier boards: upper tier—supervisory board, lower tier—management board	Executive and nonexecutive directors, latter representing outside finance more important
14	Goal of Board of Directors	To promote shareholder wealth	To promote long-term organizational health	To promote long-term organizational health
15	Executive compensation	High	Moderate	Low
16	Dividend	High	Low	Low

Following the Civil War (1861–65) US economy expanded rapidly. Many mergers took place around this time and in railways, oil, steel and other capital and technology-intensive industries (of those days), market shares started getting concentrated in a few companies. By 1850 itself, the American companies had reached a critical point in their existence: they needed large capital to expand the scale of their operations and their internal, administrative complexities were such that managerial expertise had become a key input for them. To raise capital on a large scale, the net had to be cast wide and so the general public had to be appealed to. Fragmented holdings of many small stock-holders meant that collectively shareholders were weak. Weak owners, strong managers became the dominant pattern of corporate growth in the USA.

A good example of this development was the Pennsylvania Railroad, chartered in 1846. Under its chief engineer and later President, J Edgar Thomson, the company achieved a spectacular increase in its operations from 500 to 6000 miles between 1869 and 1873. Shareholders of the company had hardly participated in choosing this course of action. In succeeding years, many other companies followed the example of Pennsylvania Railroad. In these companies, managers kept shareholders at arm's length and shareholders did not mind the distance as long as they got their dividend cheques regularly. Because of stringent listing requirements of New York stock exchange, security by rating agencies such as Moody's and Standard & Poor and government regulations to limit abuses in new security issues, share ownership became widespread.

Two types of centralization were in the USA in the later half of nineteenth century. Within a firm, there was concentration of authority in the hands of top management or just the CEO and within an industry, there was concentration of capital in a few, large firms. A survey in 1904 showed that more than 5000 independent businesses had been combined into just 300 industrial trusts. It has been hypothesized that this concentration was helped by 1 share, 1 vote norm for empowering shareholders. (Otherwise 1 person, 1 vote rule and other limitations on the voting power of large shareholders were common at that time, especially in Europe. See Chapter 3, *Appendix I* for further details.) This rule pulled out all obstacles from the path of capital and allowed it full scope for concentration. The result was that the US surged ahead in the economic field.

As businesses continued to raise capital from public, equity ownership was transferred from direct investors to portfolio investors. This enabled owner-entrepreneurs to retire from the industrial scene. Their place was taken up by ambitious, competent and visionary executives in companies such as International Harvester, General Electric and AT&T. Fragmented equity holdings gave them enough scope to earmark resources for innovation and for building organizational and technological capabilities of their companies. Retained earnings financed their investment in modern plant and technology, marketing and distribution facilities, R&D and also human resources. They followed Fordist policies after the Second World War to share their prosperity with employees and customers and they enjoyed stability and success right up to 1970s.

Banks and insurance companies were major holders of corporate bonds which got low but stable returns. By the 1960s basic economic conditions began to change because of foreign competition and rise of institutional investors. In consumer electronics, automobile and steel industries, Japanese corporations began to challenge the US business. Transfer of shareholding from individual investors to institutional investors began to weaken financial commitment to long-term organizational prosperity. Thus the way was paved for market-control perspective to emerge.

By continuously searching for higher yields, mutual funds led this process of change. Through rapid trading of large blocks of stocks and by locking in of capital gains in advance of expected stock declines, mutual fund managers tried to earn returns higher than those to be had from stable portfolios. Their success prompted pension funds and insurance companies to increase their holding of equity shares. The more institutional investors shuffled their portfolios to increase current yields, the more they subverted the commitment of finance to long-term industrial development.

Executive excesses and executive resistance of takeovers gave rise to a shareholder value movement around mid-1980s. It moved on to the UK and Europe also. After raising a lot of dust it ended in short-termism by the end of the 1990s. The movement was started by some accountants who saw that they could predict better share price movements by discounting future cash-flow streams of a business and by ignoring conventional accounting measures of performance such as earnings per share. Some aggressive bankers used this idea to raid companies whose shares were undervalued on stock exchanges. When these raids succeeded, they went on to restructure the businesses in order to tap their hidden value. They were then sold to new owners and in the process, the bankers earned large profits.

The threat from these raids caused all businesses to pay attention to the idea of shareholder value. They also started linking executive pay to their success in raising companies' stock prices. Driven by this incentive, executives too, started acting like the raiders: they cut costs, closed older plants, moved production to low-cost venues in other countries, reduced work force, outsourced all activities that outside suppliers could perform cheaply and they got rid of all underperforming parts. There is no denying that these measures led to immediate and often, spectacular results. Corporate performance improved, profits and stock prices went up and executive pay also jumped up, thanks to stock options that were given to executives.

As more and more managers were paid with stock options and as the US stock market soared in the 1990s, stock price increase became an end in itself. All managers tried to make decisions as per a single criterion – whether the outcome would cause the stock price to go still higher. So costs were cut irrespective of longrun consequences. R&D expenditure was cut back; if internal costs were found to be rigid, suppliers were squeezed to produce drastic reductions in costs as a price of continuing to do business. If these steps failed to get the necessary result on stock prices, then funds were used to buy back stock in the market. Longtime employees were forced into early retirement and interest of consumers was ignored as companies pruned their long-standing product ranges to concentrate on only the most profitable items.

Stock options of executives wrought a lot of damage. As they derived large income from stock options, the incentive to choose innovative investment strategies was weakened. Their interest became linked with market rather than organization-control. By boosting short-term profits, top managers saw the market value of their shares rise which in turn justified increasing dividends to maintain yields which reduced retained earnings.

Since top executives held shares, both ownership and control were integrated in their hands. American corporate firms managed to revive their sagging profits through re-engineering and downsizing. However, more enduring bases of competitive advantage such as new products, human capital and organization structure were ignored. Profits and stock prices of corporations continued to rise while organizational control and financial commitment were eroded.

Stakeholders reacted to these developments by applying pressure wherever they could. This led to more sober rethinking about corporate stability, corporate purpose and national competitive advantage, treatment of time factor in decision-making (focusing only on the short-run or also caring about long-run implications of current actions), contribution of other stakeholders and corporate obligations to them etc. In retrospect, it is clear that the shareholder value movement registered gains for shareholders in the short-run by ignoring long-term prospects and by sacrificing interests of other stakeholders. However, it now appears that capital market control will increasingly lean in favour of the short period and long-term organizational prospects etc. will or have already become empty terms. Any schism between long-term corporate interest and shareholder value was not considered plausible in the Anglo-American corporate governance system. Shareholder value movement has changed that.

Until recently, shareholders in the USA have been very passive, not having the will to make use of the limited power to influence management that has been granted under company law. In the 1980s, institutional investors, particularly pension funds started playing a more aggressive role. Corporate governance reforms have concentrated on the following:

- greater role for non-executive directors in holding managers accountable,
- greater use of board committees to ensure that the board discharges its responsibility,
- efforts for greater disclosure to bring about transparency,
- statutory regulation of auditors to ensure that they do not encounter conflict of interest while discharging their duty of certifying financial position of corporate firms,
- greater interest in governance of portfolio companies by public pension funds.

As mentioned above, this system is dominated today by capital market-control perspective. However, striking a golden mean between that and stakeholder-control perspective will be beneficial in future.

British Corporate Governance System

Brief Historical Background

The strongest capital market-control perspective in corporate governance is seen in the UK today. Institutional investors started becoming important in the UK since the 1960s and their continuous search for higher and higher yields from portfolio investments is reflected in high dividend pay-out rates as compared to the USA, Germany and Japan.

Since the late nineteenth century, British industry started lagging behind the American and the German industry both technologically and organizationally. This happened because there was no managerial revolution in the UK. Proprietary control of business continued in the UK far longer as compared to other countries. To meet the growing need for capital, public issues of non-voting, preference shares were common. However, retained earnings were the main source of growth for established businesses. So proprietary control remained intact.

Bank overdraft was another source of finance. However, instead of using it to smoothen out cash flow, many businesses used it for fixed capital investment. This put a lot of strain on the banking system, especially during recessions. At the same time, big British banks never provided venture capital which German banks did. Financial commitment to industry has not existed in the UK. The British financial community has taken more interest in foreign investments rather than industrial development. The separation of finance from the British industry is well known. Thus the UK has never seen organization-control perspective on corporate governance.

By the end of the 1920s, banks took a lead in industry wide rationalizations. Over-leveraged firms were amalgamated with larger businesses and owners as well as creditors of merged firms were given equity shares in the new companies. Old owners still retained decision-making authority in their hands because of their close grasp of operational details. This impeded the process of rationalization of product lines and cooperation among firms for marketing and research.

Over the years, shares in amalgamated firms changed hands on the stock exchanges and thus proprietary control of business ended. Its place was not taken by strong managers and organization-control perspective to take care of innovation and learning for sustained prosperity. By the 1940s and the 1950s, many successful firms that still had proprietary control, issued new equity shares to satisfy growing demand by portfolio investors. Non-voting, preference shares fell into disuse. Rise of institutional investors became noticeable since the late 1950s. Because the British business did not show any spectacular achievement, particularly in using and developing technology, market-control of business was soon established. Institutional investors strengthened this trend.

Pension funds were popular in the UK from the beginning of the twentieth century. By the late 1950s, management of pension funds was professionalized and competing funds tried to attract customers by promising them higher yield. Rise of institutional investors and market-control perspective on corporate governance have been linked together.

German Corporate Governance System

Brief Historical Background

Organization-control is the dominant corporate governance perspective in Germany. Non-financial corporate firms rather than banks and financial institutions are the most important block holders of equity in Germany. The corporate governance system consists of a network of institutional arrangements such as company law, co-determination law, proxy voting system, cross holdings and stock exchange regulations etc.

Company law in Germany provides for a two-tier board structure in which there is no overlapping between the two tiers. Premature removal of members of both supervisory and management boards is prohibited. The boards are expressly asked to act in the interest of the corporation and not shareholders. Similarly takeover bids financed by the assets of target firms are prohibited.

The Co-determination Act, 1951 requires that half of the seats of the supervisory board be occupied by workers in iron, steel and coal industries. Otherwise the proportion is one-third of the total seats. Under the proxy voting system, banks vote on behalf of their clients and are therefore important block holders.

In the nineteenth century, the German companies also found it necessary to tap the general public for raising capital. However, instead of issuing shares to the public, public savings with banks were tapped. So banks have been important in corporate governance system and block holders have always been powerful.

At the same time, at the beginning of the twentieth century, major companies such as Siemens and Thyssen consolidated their market positions without bank finance. They relied almost exclusively on retained earnings. Other companies used bank finance with retained earnings but instead of relying on only one bank, they used a number of banks so as to avoid the stronghold of finance capital.

In the last part of the nineteenth century, concentration of capital started taking place in different industries. Cartels and other loose combinations rather than mergers were preferred and so small firms continued to exist in the market. In their internal working also, the German companies stuck to 1 person, 1 vote rule rather than 1 share, 1 vote rule, a little longer as compared to the USA.

By 1910, managerial revolution had taken place in the German industry. Independent financial positions of large companies were strengthened during the World War I on the basis of government orders which generated huge profits. After the war, their independence increased further as they managed to protect the value of their assets from the ravages of inflation. After the war, inter-business linkages became tight. To counter an adverse situation caused by military defeat and demands for repatriation payments, German industries formed massive concerns called Konzerne. These were organizations in which one main company took a long-term shareholding in a number of other companies for the purpose of coordinating their financial and investment strategies. This process created a dense web of interlocking shareholdings and directorships that increased managerial control of these companies relative to that of shareholders/financial institutions.

During mid-1930s and the early 1940s, Nazis strengthened inter-company linkages. With Germany's defeat in World War II, allied forces wanted to break the concentration of economic power in German industry and banking. Three major commercial banks were divided by the Allied forces but they reconsolidated. However, with the onset of the Cold War, the Allied goal shifted to making the German economy strong as a bulwark against the rising Soviet power.

In the 1980s, when capital market-control was becoming dominant in the USA and the UK, the German companies were restructuring their financial relations so as to strengthen organization-control. Around 1985, a number of listed, large companies issued new shares, mostly to acquire shares of other companies rather than to finance the formation of new assets. Large companies also used their financial reserves to lend funds to smaller companies with which they had business connections, thus strengthening inter-company linkages, often taking away loan business from bank.

However, now the trend is towards liberalization of equity market and financial sector has greater incentives to extract higher yields through portfolio investment rather than maintain a commitment to productive investment. The German banks are taking a fresh look at their stakes in German companies. Shareholders have begun challenging voting rights restrictions. More stringent rules against insider trading are in the offing. A beginning towards shareholder rights movement has been made and higher dividends, greater transparency are being demanded.

A solid alliance between finance and industrial capital has been the main feature of the German corporate governance. Because of the enormous clout of banks till now, activism of other shareholders has been futile. Debate in corporate governance in Germany centers around the rights of minority shareholders. In 1995, some governance standards were introduced to protect minority shareholders' interests in the event of a takeover. A takeover commission has also been established to monitor the implementation of these standards. All in all, this system has now started leaning towards the Anglo-American system.

Japanese Corporate Governance System

Brief Historical Background

Heavy reliance on trust, implicit contracting and a relationship-oriented approach are the main features of this system. There exists a close tie-up between banks and industry. Inter-corporate cross-holdings are prominent and hostile takeovers are very difficult. There is concentration on long-term company interest, long-term investment in employee training and R&D which have given a competitive edge to Japanese firms.

Organization-control is the hallmark of Japanese corporate governance, too. Roots of organization-control in Japan go back to the Meiji Restoration of 1868. In the 1870s, postal savings system was mobilized in Japan to avoid borrowing foreign capital. It placed household savings in the hands of the government which made them available to private banks that were interested in financing industries. The government ensured that banks provided these funds for long-term investment in industries. Banks retained the right to call back the money lent to industry on the understanding that this money was committed for long-term. With this relationship with banks, industrial enterprises had very high debt-equity ratios. The proportion of retained earnings was also high and thus industrial development began against the backdrop of committed finance.

Some of the banks were a part of *zaibatsu* – the family-owned holding companies. In some sectors e.g. railways and cotton textiles, *zaibatsu* did not play an important role but wealthy merchants did. Their financial position was fragile but they employed university educated engineers. Due to their development of human capital they later found it easier to have access to the funds of *zaibatsu* banks. Successful *zaibatsu* families functioned as venture capitalists and a stock market was non-existent prior to the World War II.

After the war, the Allied occupation dissolved the *zaibatsu* by distributing shares in holding companies to the general public. So trading in equity became important for the first time in Tokyo Stock Exchange. In the 1950s, after the departure of Allies, the Japanese business community, led by top managers of major industrial companies and banks, initiated a cross-holding movement to ensure that outside shareholders did not disrupt the working of industries such as automobiles and consumer electronics. Japanese business bought blocks of each other's shares with the intent of remaining stable shareholders who would neither sell the shares in the market nor demand high dividends. (Business groups are now called *keiretsu*.) Thus organization-control was facilitated and providing permanent employment and high earnings to employees became major enterprise goals. After Japan joined the OECD in 1964, Japanese businesses increased their cross-holdings to make sure that foreigners did not, through the secondary capital market, take over successful Japanese businesses. Even today, cross-holdings account for the biggest chunk of outstanding equity in Japan. It is as though the Japanese business community has undertaken, through cross-holdings, to suspend the rights of traditional property ownership for the sake of long-term growth of Japanese economy.

Until recently, the foundation of corporate finance in Japan has retained earnings which have been highly leveraged by loans from banks. Organization control remains dominant in Japan because of two reasons viz.

1. Business community has agreed that shareholders cannot extract resources from enterprises.
2. Government regulation of the financial system has ensured that debt financing would be secure and inexpensive.

Recently, more mergers and acquisitions are seen in Japan. Competition in the capital market is increasing and so there is greater pressure on financial institutions to seek greater returns in the short-term. In the past, Japan's institutional investors including banks and life insurance companies were not keen to exercise their influence on corporate managements unless they were facing financial or other difficulties. Their influence tended to be mainly behind the scenes. Now investors are becoming less accommodating and institutional investors are realizing the importance of maximum shareholder value as the goal of corporate governance. In other words, Americanization of Japanese corporate governance is taking place.

(The Indian corporate governance system which is an amalgam of the Anglo-American and the German, the Japanese systems is discussed in Chapters 5 and 8.)

Table 2.3. *Comparative performance of different corporate governance systems*

Attributes	Anglo-American system	German system	Japanese system
Strengths	1 dynamic, market-based 2 liquid capital 3 internationalization non-problematic	1 long-term industrial strategy 2 stable capital 3 strong overseas investment governance procedures	1 long-term industrial strategy 2 stable capital
Weaknesses	1 instability 2 short-termism	1 internationalization difficult 2 vulnerable to global capital market	1 secretive, corrupt practices 2 growth in institutional activism and financial speculation in recent times

Thus given the historical development and the complexity of issues involved, there is no consensus as to which is the best corporate governance system. Macey (1998) suggests that different systems should be compared on the basis of their empirical performance vis-a-vis these criteria:

1 How well do they restrict managers' ability to divert corporate resources to private use?
2 How much do firms tend to go public under them? Firms that operate under an efficient corporate governance system will be able to sell their shares to the public while inefficient corporate governance system will not be able to offer this advantage.
3 How quickly are under-performing managements replaced? Is the replacement effected through internal or external means?

Conclusion

The brief and sketchy account of the evolution of corporate governance systems as given above underscores some very important points. They are:

1 Shareholders have not been given the most privileged position in corporate governance systems. While block holders remain important, small shareholders have been taken for granted and ignored till capital market becomes dominant.
2 Managers and other stakeholders have been important to varying degrees.
3 Separation between ownership and control of capital is a basic feature of only the Anglo-American corporate governance system.
4 Experimentation with orthodox notions of ownership has been continuously carried out in corporate governance systems. Traditional concepts of property rights have been changed to boost economic development.
5 There exists a close linkage between financial and corporate governance systems. Corporate governance system is a part of the financial system. Hence its nature changes depending on whether the latter is bank-based or market-based.
6 Organization-control perspective is important in an economy which is trying to create a corporate governance system, which will promote industrial development. It is a necessary but insufficient condition for industrial development.
7 Corporate governance system is firmly linked to the process of skill formation in an economy. Training of people in organizations is important if they are to make innovative decisions. A corporate governance system cannot remain oblivious to this aspect.

Finally, it must be emphasized that different economies have evolved their corporate governance systems to suit their circumstances. If this evolution process is to continue, individual businesses must have flexibility to change in a manner they consider appropriate. However, today there is a broad tendency towards convergence of different systems because of globalization of capital. In a global capital market, investors will give preference to transparent and investor-friendly businesses. More and better disclosures and giving effective voice option to shareholders will become increasingly important in days to come all over the world.

3

Anglo-American Corporate Governance System

Anglo-American corporate governance system can be understood only in the context of a competitive capital market. Basic tenets of this system are:
1 Managers are separate from shareholders. So shareholders can easily sell and buy shares in the stock exchange.
2 Shareholders' interference in management is to be avoided provided managers manage firms in the interest of shareholders.
3 Managers will have clear information about shareholders' expectations and shareholders will have enough information to judge whether their expectations are being met or not. This information-exchange will take place primarily in the form of stock prices.

This system is a many-layered arrangement of parts which are both internal and external to a firm. The first part is the Board of Directors which has to be sensitive to the changing circumstances and changing perceptions and expectations of shareholders. Large shareholders usually appoint their representative to the board. Small, dispersed shareholders do not enjoy this facility and so the second part emphasizes adequate disclosure and transparency in communicating with them. The third layer, is occupied by auditors who report to shareholders about firm performance. The fourth layer, provides for the exercise of voting rights of shareholders and for raising their collective voice over contentious issues through proxy fights. This internal arrangement is designed to give 'voice' to investors.

Capital market directly supplements this arrangement. Stock prices indicate investors' assessment of firm performance and by disposing off their shares, shareholders can communicate their displeasure to managers. Similarly, investors and entrepreneurs notify management about its under-performance through a takeover bid. The stock exchange gives 'exit' option to investors.

Till the 1990s, exit option dominated voice option in Anglo-American corporate governance. Thus shareholders have preferred to sell their shares quietly in case of businesses they have been unhappy with. Of course, for this arrangement to work effectively, capital market itself has to function efficiently and stock price must be flexible to reflect firm performance accurately.

This system functions in a framework of competitive product markets and a politico-legal institutional set-up that protects investors' rights. Indeed, it has been said that provided the framework is right, the system corrects itself automatically and policy-makers do not have to interfere with its individual parts. Thus the failure of internal arrangement in the 1980s was corrected by the spate of hostile takeover bids in the stock exchange. Efficient markets are enough to set the system right, avers this view. Its opponents have pointed out that this means waking up too late after much damage has taken place and large amounts of capital and other resources have got wasted in the process. Therefore corporate governance is a credible area for policy prescription.

Actual functioning of this system will now be examined under the following headings:
1 Board of directors structure
2 Executive compensation
3 Ownership structure
4 Financial structure.
The institutional set-up will be examined under the following heads:
1 Disclosure of information
2 Voting rights
3 Proxy contests
4 Takeovers and takeover defenses.

Board of Directors: structure

Whether the board is unitary or multi-tier and in the former case, the proportion of executive and non-executive directors are matters which are supposed to be very important in governance. Inclusion of non-executive directors is expected to bring independent thinking and breadth of vision to bear upon a firm's problems and it is also thought that overall quality of direction would improve as internal control mechanism would be strengthened. Cadbury Committee recommended a great role for these directors in monitoring firm performance. This recommendation has been widely accepted. Then the board is expected to discharge its responsibilities by appointing various committees of which audit committee is the main one.

Critics question the onerous responsibility that is being heaped upon them. They point out that it is naive to expect directors who are chosen by managers to monitor the performance of the same managers objectively. According to Jensen, only the capital market can discharge such a responsibility.

Since the Cadbury report a lot of research has been undertaken in regard to various facets of board functioning. On the whole, available evidence on the relationship between board structure and board effectiveness is positive.

Executive Compensation

Corporate governance movement started in the USA because of shareholders' complaints about excessive executive pay. There were many cases of firms which had reported poor operational results but their managers had taken home a very generous compensation packet.

It has been stated earlier that executive remuneration tends to be low in Japan, moderate in Germany, high in the UK and highest in the USA. So the press, business analysts and shareholders in the USA are always interested in this issue.

Actually, if managers' rewards could vary with firm performance, much of the agency problem would be solved. Managers would only try to maximize their earnings but in the process they would also maximize shareholder value. This is an old idea and so managers' compensation comprises several parts including salary, commission based on profit, bonus and stock options. Executive bonuses and stock options were earlier based on accounting measures of firm performance. Now firm performance is measured in terms of stock prices. This did not make much difference in the 1970s as stock price movements in the USA were then few. Now however, they can bring about volatile movements in compensation amounts. Executives have been very innovative in trying to ensure that they do not.

Jensen and Murphy (1990) found that executive pay changed by $3 for every $1000 change in the wealth of a firm. This seemingly small elasticity of executive pay can of course have a considerable impact on executives' net worth in absolute terms.

Stock options have become very popular of late but as mentioned earlier, not everybody is in favour of them. Capital market and stakeholder-control perspectives favour them. Organization-control perspective adopts an ambivalent stand on them while shareholder control-perspective singles them out as the chief culprit of the present problem of Anglo-American corporate governance system.

The widely-held view about the link between executive pay and performance of the firm is that there is no strong relation between the two. This means that executives have written their compensation packages in such a way that they continue to receive handsome pay packages irrespective of the state of firm's affairs. In other words, the individual components of their pay move up or down but the sum always leaves them comfortably off. In spite of the instant attention it attracts, this measure does not have much scope for reducing agency costs and is not a very important issue in corporate governance discussion.

Ownership Structure

Shareholding of a corporate firm can be widely diffused or concentrated in the hands of a few individuals or institutions. The former makes the firm a widely-held corporation and the latter, closely-held. The thesis of Berle and Means was that all corporations would eventually be widely held. That is not happening. In the USA, small shareholders did emerge as the largest group of owners in the early 1970s but institutional owners have taken their place since then. In the rest of the countries in the world, both developed and developing, there has always existed significant concentration of shareholding and the situation is likely to continue for a long time to come.

Large shareholders usually have their representatives on the Board of Directors and they maintain a close relationship with the top management of the investee company. Befitting their large stake in the firm, they ensure that they have good and up-to-date information about both the inside environment and external factors affecting the firm. Such close ties help in reducing agency costs but they lead to expropriation of minority shareholders and they may bring down the incentive of managers to strive for excellence. Close monitoring by owners goes against the spirit of managerial professionalism. Expropriation of minority shareholder interest may mean drying up of alternative sources of finance to the firm.

There exist two opposite tendencies of the effect of ownership concentration on company performance. The covergence of interest tendency is for increase in company value as shareholders' and firm's interests get closely aligned. Entrenchment tendency is opposite: because of concentrated shareholding, particular shareholders get entrenched and they can ignore other shareholders and also block takeover bids. Such a situation leads to a divergence between firm interest and shareholder interest and then it leads to a drop in company value. If convergence tendency is more prominent, greater concentration of shareholding will add value and dominance of entrenchment tendency, will lead to a decline in company value. It is also possible that as concentration level starts rising, company value will increase initially and decline after a point when disadvantages of entrenchment outweigh all other advantages.

Indeed, a study by Morck, Shleifer and Vishny (1988) tried to relate company performance to insider ownership and it found that as ownership concentration increased from 0 to 5 per cent, company performance improved. As concentration went beyond that point up to 25 per cent, performance deteriorated and beyond 25 per cent, again there was improvement in performance, albeit (it was) slow. The study therefore concluded that between ownership range of 0–5 per cent, convergence of interest between block holders and the firm took place. Between 5 and 25 per cent, entrenchment effect was prominent and it reduced company performance. Again his adverse effect was slowly offset as concentration increased beyond 25 per cent and convergence of interest predominated. Sarkar and Sarkar replicated this study in India. They correlated the performance and ownership structure of 1567 companies in 1995–96 and found that block holding had a positive impact on company value.

On the whole, available evidence points out that majority ownership is viable. Institutional investors are also expected to add value. However, they can usher in short-termism and conflicts of interest prevent them from playing an active role in corporate governance, except on a selective basis. The role of institutional investors is explored in detail in Chapter 7.

Financial Structure

Financial structure of a firm basically refers to the equity and debt in its capitalization. The pure theory of finance has held that creditors have nothing to do with corporate governance as long as the firm makes no default in interest payment. Hence financial structure ought not to matter in corporate governance.

In reality, creditors – particularly large creditors – do make a difference. Large creditors may mediate in major operational decisions and a firm will accept the arrangement because it may have to, time and again, tap them to raise more funds. Creditors' association with a firm reaches its zenith when their nominees are appointed to the board. In Germany and Japan, approximately 75 and 50 per cent of large companies respectively, have a commercial banker on their board. In India too, public financial institutions have hitherto enjoyed a direct right of participation in corporate governance. Of course, they have combined the roles of *creditors* as well as *shareholders* in many of the businesses. We can generalize by stating that in bank-based financial systems, large creditors are an important constituent of corporate governance. In capital market-based financial system also, large creditors play a part, albeit in a selective, closed door fashion. Therefore creditors matter in corporate governance and a debt instrument can be made effective in reducing agency costs.

Large creditors have professional expertise and experience in screening firm performance. They enjoy wide exposure to a variety of situations, markets and industries. They can help in reducing costs of financial distress. For example, a study of 121 Japanese firms, found that firms in distress which had financial institutions as creditors invested more and had more robust sales performance than non-group firms in the years following the onset of difficulties.

Institutional Framework

Corporate governance mechanism is an institutional mechanism and its working is the outcome of legal and political decisions. Thus shareholders' control of management depends upon their voting and proxy rights as defined in company law. Creditors' ability to press financial claims on a bankrupt company depends upon bankruptcy laws and takeover rules decide how far they will be effective in disciplining errant corporations.

The legal and political environment works in a different fashion as compared to the economic environment that is largely market-based. Changes in the former are slow and they have to have democratic sanction. The problem of providing checks on company management is like the problem of causing elected representatives to be responsive to the electorate in a political democracy. Shareholders' rights are even more unexercised as compared to citizens'. That is so because corporate democracy is a one-party system. Management, not shareholders, selects a single group of candidates, controls the proxy machinery and also the campaign funds. While citizens vote on the basis of matters they all understand and have opinions on e.g. taxes and subsidies, civil rights, foreign policy etc., corporate citizens are not able to judge the soundness of corporate policies except in extraordinary cases. Therefore management becomes entrenched and comes to possess self-perpetuating power. USA provides a legal remedy called **derivative suit** to shareholders. It is an action brought in the name of the corporation to redress any wrong. Normally, courts do not, second guess management. They defer to its *'business judgement'* rule. If a corporate firm is injured by mismanagement or abuse of position that falls outside the business judgement rule, any shareholder can sue the management on behalf of the corporation. The scope of derivative suit is confined to flagrant wrongs that the Board of Directors could not ratify by a valid exercise of its business judgement.

In a landmark case in the USA in 1919, the Dodge brothers, important shareholders, had sued the Ford Motor Company with the allegation that Henry Ford who controlled the Board of Directors of the company, was not sufficiently concerned with the welfare of its shareholders. After paying $1.2 million in dividends on a capital of $2 million, Henry Ford had decided to suspend future dividend payments indefinitely. At the time, the company was retaining $58 million in profits for expanding business and for cutting down costs. The Dodge brothers asserted that shareholders owned the company and they were entitled to force directors to payout some of their accumulated profit. The court upheld their view and asked Ford to payout dividends as demanded by Dodge brothers. Thus at that time, no possibility of conflict of interest between a corporate body and its shareholders was admitted. The situation has changed considerably now. The corporate body is routinely assumed to have an independent existence and disputes break out over who represents corporate interests – managers or shareholders? The difference between organization-control and shareholder-control perspectives of corporate governance arises precisely on this score. Derivative suit is one more manifestation of the same difference.

Between 1875 and 1918, Clarence H. Venner had brought a number of derivative suits against well-known American corporations. Nowadays a restriction called security for expenses is placed on shareholders if they wish to file such a suit. The restriction stipulates that the plaintiff must execute a bond unless he holds 5 per cent or $ 50,000 worth of stock. In Baker v/s Macfadden Publications Inc. (1946, N.Y.) the plaintiff owned less than 1 per cent of stock the market value of which was less than \$350 but he wanted to file a derivative suit and he tried to obtain a list of other shareholders to garner support. He was not permitted to do either.

We will now take a closer look at the institutional framework of corporate governance with reference to four parameters viz. disclosure of information, voting rights of shareholders, proxy contests and takeover defenses.

Disclosure of Information

Transparency is highly valued in the global capital market and so a trend towards greater disclosure of information can be seen everywhere. It is believed that 'sunlight is the best disinfectant.' Of course, there are many imperfections and there is a long way to go. However, matters were different in this respect until recently. Since the exit rather than voice option was emphasized, there was a widespread feeling that shareholders were not entitled to know more than the bare minimum, that any information (even about sales) was valuable to competitors and so should be kept under wraps. In India, in one annual general meeting of Voltas Ltd., the board chairman, Mr A.H.T. Tobaccowala, actually refused to answer a shareholder who kept asking a number of questions and advised him to sell his shares and be content with assured good return.

In an efficient capital market, the real and perceived value of a security tend to stay together. Security price is influenced more by conjecture and perception rather than real value. Still, if enough information is available, security price mirrors real worth, notwithstanding temporary deviations between the two.

If adequate information is not available, security price gets delinked from real value and becomes volatile. Many a time, poor information flow is characterized also by asymmetry of information. This means that one type of investors is better informed than others. It compounds the problem and security price starts fluctuating wildly. To avoid this volatility, a continuous or regular flow of information from a firm is necessary. It enables investors to arrive at better judgement of the firm and fairer price for its securities.

Companies that are performing well and also those that fare poorly need to disclose information regularly to investors. In case of companies that are doing well, such disclosure serves to build confidence about consistency and credibility of performance. Poorly performing companies can inform investors about their proposed corrective measures and this information may stall a decline in their share price. Since everyone wants to talk about success and is tight-lipped about failure and mistakes, regular disclosure in adverse times earns respect for a company.

Disclosure of information by a firm is of two types. The first is one-time disclosure in the primary market at the time of issuing securities. The second is regular disclosure in the secondary market regarding firm performance and future prospects. Both are important but in discussing the role of disclosure in corporate governance, it is primarily regular disclosure that matters.

Charkham and Simpson opine that information to be disclosed to shareholders should relate to four 'P's – performance, position (relative market position), people (functions, track record and qualifications of directors, top managers) and prospects or outlook for future performance. Information that a firm wants to give and information that investors want are generally two different things. For example, the firm wants to talk about projects likely to be completed soon while investors want to focus on cost and time overruns. Management wants to stress new product features but investors want to know break-even point and additional sales revenue. Management is keen to talk about synergy following a merger while investors want to look at increase in promoters' ownership share after the merger. Management focuses on growth in profit but investors are worried about lack of sales growth and so on.

Regular disclosure of information brings about the following benefits:

1 More information about company performance means more accurate share prices which enable the secondary capital market to perform its task of limiting agency costs more efficiently. More realistic share prices make threats of hostile takeovers more real. So capital market becomes more fair and efficient.

2 Accurate share prices also mean accurate cost of capital, particularly when a firm contemplates financing a new investment project entirely through the sale of shares. Price of one source of capital affects all other sources through relative prices. On the demand side, they affect the preference of management between debt and equity and enable it to move closer to the optimum financial structure. Without it, management might take up unpromising investment projects, buoyed up high public perceptions which are a result of erroneously high share prices. If on the other hand, share prices are inaccurately low, the firm might have to give up legitimate investment projects because of a constraint of both external and internal funds.

3 More realistic share price can increase the use of share-price based executive compensation. As has already been mentioned, this can potentially help in reducing agency costs by bringing managers' interests closer to those of shareholders. If share prices are distorted, there is greater risk in this type of compensation, from managers' viewpoint. The role of share-price based executive compensation in corporate governance is a controversial point.

4 Accounting measures of a firm's performance have now become outdated and greater use is being made of share-price based measures. It is imperative therefore that share prices reflect the firm performance accurately. Greater regular disclosure is therefore in keeping with the general trend of change.

5 Shareholders are able to exercise their voting rights effectively. Greater information with small shareholders may not lead to any action while with large stakeholders, it means a decisive change. Analysis of more, better information placed at their disposal is likely to enhance the interest of all investors as greater information enables them to make rational decisions.

6 There are substantial economies of scale when certain information is prepared and issued to all shareholders. It would be costly to prepare and give information to individual shareholders according to their particular needs. Further, such information will not be public. In all countries, trading on the basis of insider/non-public information is prohibited. Therefore mandatory, enhanced disclosure is beneficial.

7 Regular disclosure also helps to improve managerial performance simply by making managers aware of various relevant aspects. Many managers, in smaller companies may be just ignorant of important, relevant points for decision-making. Rules for enhanced disclosure will force this awareness on them and enhance the quality of their decision- making. They may also force managers to confront disagreeable reality early on. This is a non-trivial point in the sense mandatory provisions are not just regulatory measures; they also serve as guidelines about best behaviour and expectations in that regard.

8 Poor transparency adversely affects liquidity of securities market.

9 Investors invest more confidently when there is greater transparency as they can distinguish good firms from bad ones.

10 Fear of exposure brings down the degree of wrongdoing by managers and it makes regulators more alert.

11 Government actions such as closing a bankrupt bank do not invite the charge of impropriety when information is there for all to see and check.

These advantages are coupled with some negative effects. (Otherwise the degree of disclosure would have been far greater than at present.) These negative aspects are:

1 It will lead some companies to give up external sources of finance and rely entirely on internal ones. This is an undesirable tendency since external finance forces managers to subject their investment choices to the scrutiny of capital market. When firms rely only on internal finance, their autonomy is taken exception to by both government and capital market.

2 Managers who work in the glare of public scrutiny, start taking actions that show them in a good light rather than actions which are in the best interests of their firms. Thus window dressing starts.

3 Incumbent managers always argue that retail investors cannot understand the complexities of a firm's finances. Actually stock exchanges have enormous sophistication in impounding information into prices but managers cling to above implicit belief which incidentally, is shared by all in power.

Voting Rights of Shareholders

As owners of a company, shareholders receive the following rights:

1 Right to receive dividend when it is declared by the Board of Directors.

2 Right to retain their proportional ownership in the company (pre-emptive right).

3   Right to inspect accounting records and books. Today this means the right to receive audited financial statements.

4   Right to receive a list of all shareholders of the company. (This is the most difficult right to exercise and usually it requires a court order. For the extraordinary general meeting of public sector – Bank of India on October 10, 2002, convened to elect 4 directors from amongst shareholders, a list of shareholders was made available to those who wished to contest the election, at a nominal charge of Rs. 40,000!)

5   Right to vote which is the most important right. Shareholders do not take part in the day-to-day affairs of a company. However, to exercise control they need to:

a   approve the company charter and byelaws before the company begins its operations

b   elect the Board of Directors

c   approve or disapprove actions of the board.

In all these cases, the task is accomplished by voting. In addition, shareholders have the right to transfer their shares, to receive information on important happenings, to elect or to approve auditors, to nominate members to the board etc.

Voting rights of shareholders play an important part in corporate governance. In a sense, corporate governance is nothing but the sum total of arrangements that are evolved to reduce agency costs. By reserving some issues for voting by shareholders, managerial discretion is limited. A going business has to adapt to changes in the market and this is reflected in its policies. In a widely held company, it is not possible to seek fresh mandate from shareholders for each such change. Such an approach would also give veto power to every shareholder. It is much more convenient to grant them voting rights, place the proposed changes in policies before them in a meeting and ask them to vote on them.

Since the right to vote is a basic right, shareholders are entitled to vote by proxy i.e. they can assign the right to another person for a certain meeting, a certain resolution or in general.

In reality, shareholders experience number of difficulties in exercising their voting rights. Small shareholders experience them more acutely. As a remarked earlier, the present corporate democracy is similar to a one-party political system. There exists only one team of directors, chosen by incumbent management, for election in the AGM. Campaign funds and proxy machinery are also controlled by management. For want of a viable alternative, shareholders take the easy way out by concurring with management proposals. In most of the cases, judging the soundness of managerial policies is difficult for small, outside shareholders.

In the case of a company with diffused, widely held shares, shareholders face the problem of collective action. Gathering more information about managerial performance and business prospects in order to vote intelligently is beneficial to all shareholders. However, individually a shareholder finds that the cost of adopting such an activist course exceeds the possible future benefits, particularly when the shareholder owns only a tiny fraction of total share capital and cannot have a decisive influence on any resolution. Even reading notices, reports and attending AGMs requires spending some time while there is no assured return. The problem is free-riding: passive shareholders do not bear costs of activism but share any benefits that result from it. As long as a mechanism for making all shareholders bear the costs does not exist, individual shareholders prefer not to take voting seriously and maintain a policy of **rational ignorance**. Free-riding afflicts proxy contests also and reduces their effectiveness as a governance tool. For example, small shareholders have less incentive to find out which competing management team is likely to add more value.

Shareholders can be meaningfully classified as small holders and block holders. The latter have greater stake in a company and they are also surer of influencing outcomes of resolutions in a certain direction. Therefore they are more forthright about incurring costs of activism as compared to small shareholders.

Perhaps even more meaningful is the distinction between **inside** and **outside shareholders**. Inside shareholders are original entrepreneurs or promoters. They often team with management and with a small portion of total share capital; abrogate the status of controlling owners. This leads to further loss of power by small, diffused shareholders.

With the induction of outside shareholders, constraint of funds goes away and this enhances company value. At the same time, diffused ownership makes managers powerful and agency costs go up. This reduces company value. Collusion of management and inside shareholders pushes up agency cost even further for outside shareholders and makes governance difficult from their point of view. This is a common situation in Indian businesses.

Outside shareholders do have some remedies for gaining a measure of control in the face of above odds. Derivative suits have already been mentioned. Another possible remedy is to change voting rules in favour of outside shareholders. For instance, the present *one share, one vote* norm might be replaced by *one person, one vote* rule as in cooperatives. This was indeed the practice two centuries ago for keeping company interest separate from that of large shareholders (See *Appendix I*). Any such attempt today will amount to reinventing the wheel. However, some modification of voting rules in favour of small shareholders is feasible and can be tried out. The trend of actual events is, on the other hand, tilted against them. We can expect further erosion in the clout of small shareholders through the issue of nonvoting shares and shares with differential voting rights.

One more interesting remedy for small shareholders has been proposed. (Baums, Randow, 1994) It involves appointing voting agents for creating informed, coordinated voting power among small shareholders. This suggestion has been made after observing German corporate governance system in which banks act as proxies for clients whose shares they hold in depository accounts. Their own and clients' shares give the German banks substantial voting power: more than 75 per cent of total votes in 100 top public limited companies in 1992. The banks generally support management proposals but should they decide to differ, they have the power to see the changes through. The German banks have exerted a remarkably stabilizing influence on the governance system.

The proposal for voting agents seeks to adopt this idea to the reality of the Anglo-American governance system. It is to operate in the following manner:

Voting agents will be professionals with finance/audit background so that they understand the reality of business. At the same time, they must not have any business links with a particular company and its shareholders. They have to offer their services to the shareholders of a particular company in a detailed offer document, state their fees and on that basis, shareholders will elect an agent from competing offers in an AGM.

The elected voting agents will represent all shareholders except those who are present to cast vote in meetings and those who have nominated their proxies. Thus 100 per cent shareholder representation will be ensured in any meeting. In order to get elected, an agent will have to secure minimum 5 per cent of the total votes cast. Two or more agents can work together in the same company depending upon its ownership structure. Elected agents will work for an agreed, fixed tenure of say, 3 years.

Voting agents will declare in advance how they plan to vote on the issues listed in the agenda of a meeting. It is expected that by employing professional analysts, the agents will carry out a serious study of concerned resolutions and also of company performance in the context of general economic and industrial performance and then crystallize their stand. If any shareholder wants to vote differently, he/she is free to do so by attending the meeting or by giving necessary instructions to the proxy. The company will pay for the services of voting agents and a separate regulatory authority will supervise their working. (Proxy contests on the other hand, are fought on the basis of private funds of shareholders.)

This proposal is expected to give collective voting strength to small, dispersed shareholders and to empower them without abridging their normal voting rights. Since voting agents will be paid by the company, all shareholders – block holders included – will share their fees and free-riding will be avoided.

Voting agents will facilitate block voting by small shareholders who will then be able to play an active role in corporate governance like institutional investors. In due course of time, with aspiring voting agents competing with each other, a market for voting rights will emerge. Block voting sans block holding facilitated by this practice can potentially have a significant effect on corporate monitoring.

Voting By Proxy and Proxy Contests

Proxy means assigning voting rights to another person. This assignment may be specific i.e. applicable at a particular meeting, to a particular resolution or it may be general – applicable to all meetings held within a certain time period.

Rules regarding voting by proxy differ from country to country. In the UK every person, who is entitled to attend and vote in a general meeting can appoint another person (member or non-member) to vote by proxy in his place. Every general body meeting notice must contain a statement of member's right to appoint proxy. If a group of shareholders wishes to mobilize the support of other shareholders for its proposals, it can solicit proxy appointments from them and use their votes in addition to its own.

In France, a proxy to be used by a shareholder may either be his/her spouse or another shareholder. Voting by mail is permitted. However, small shareholders owning less than 10 shares may not be permitted to attend AGM. In Germany, voting by mail is prohibited. A proxy may be given to a shareholder or a bank or shareholders' association. Most of the German banks offer the service of voting for depositors' shares. Custodian banks are empowered to ask their clients for standing proxies which remain valid for up to 15 months but can be revoked by the shareholder any time. In the absence of specific instructions by the shareholder, a bank can vote at its discretion in the best interest of the shareholder. This is a major reason for banks' large influence over corporate affairs in Germany. Attempts made so far to limit this influence have been ineffective. In the Netherlands, shareholders have to vote either in person or by proxy. The Dutch Shareholders' Association often acts as a proxy for its members and other shareholders. In India, shareholders can vote by proxy and voting by mail has been introduced only recently as per The Companies (Amendment) Act, 2000. Postal ballot is to be sought by companies for specified matters only. If each and every resolution in the AGM were to be voted in person or through post then voting by proxy might become superfluous.

A proxy contest refers to the use of shareholders' votes at company meetings in order to influence incumbent management, to pass favourable resolutions or to replace management. It is a political campaign in which shareholders who disagree with managerial policies seek election to board of directors and is an assertion of their right to sack incumbent management. During the contest, dissidents paint a broad picture of incumbent's incompetence and cite poor operating performance, excessive managerial compensation, unsatisfactory dividends, low share ownership by the current board and general unreliability of management etc. Incumbent management stoutly defends itself. However, the campaign tends to over-simplify the issues because of the problem of free-riding i.e. small incentive for individual shareholders to find out which team will add more value. Therefore some experts have opined that proxy contests are a less efficient corporate governance mechanism than tender offers and mergers.

Companies which have proxy contests typically have less-than-market rate of return. As news of a contests reaches the share market, share price goes up because it is expected that the contest will either install a better team of managers in the company or serve to make the existing team more efficient. Often a link exists between proxy contests and takeovers via tender offers: the former are a part of a potential acquirer's takeover strategy. Proxy contests are convenient when takeover defences erected by management and stringent takeover laws make tender offers very expensive. In other words, limited resources with dissident shareholders or corporate bidders induce them to seek control of the target firm by soliciting votes from other shareholders rather than purchasing shares outright.

Legally, a proxy contest can be successful even when it manages to put just 2 members of the dissident group on the Board of Directors. One of them can propose a motion and the other seconds it. Then the motion will be in the minutes of the board meeting and other directors will take note of it. Actually many proxy fights are unable to get a majority on the board. These fights are expensive and shareholders have to finance them from their own funds. (If successful, these shareholders later manage to reimburse themselves for the costs.)

It was found that in around 25 to 33 per cent of proxy contests, dissidents managed to elect a majority of directors and in less than 20 per cent of companies whose managers were busy with proxy contests, the same management team was found 3 years after the contest. Thus even unsuccessful proxy contests serve to remove incumbent management either directly or via sale of the company.

In short, proxy contests are more effective in disciplining management than would be indicated by the incidence of dissidents actually gaining control of the board. Nevertheless, certain limitations in the voting or regulatory process (e.g. incumbents use company money to fight dissidents) render them a less effective corporate governance mechanism.

Takeovers and Takeover Defenses

Marris is credited with the first theory of takeovers and their impact on corporate governance. The threat of takeovers forces managers to opt for high dividend payout and this results in a short-term orientation which is harmful to organizational interest, he averred. J.E. Meade (1968) thought that by changing a slack management, takeovers enabled a firm to increase company value. He clarified that many small, diffused shareholders would be unable to mount a takeover threat but a large company or institution might make a generous bid to shareholders, acquire a majority of shares and then enforce a change in management. This would cause company value to increase and then the block holder would reap a large benefit.

According to Jensen (1986), agency costs associated with management – shareholder conflict over the payout of free cash flow are a major cause of takeovers. Free cash flow, is cash flow in excess of amounts required to fund all projects that have positive net present values when discounted appropriately. If the firm is to be efficient and if share price is to be maximized, such free cash should be handed over to shareholders by managers. However, this decreases the discretionary resources available with managers and also their power. Plus, for new investment opportunities, they have to take recourse to capital market and be subject to its monitoring. So managers try to retain free cash. The resultant conflict between shareholders' interest and managers' interest invites takeover bids.

Takeovers result in a rise in company value on the following counts:

1   Efficiency improves whenever firms with unequal managerial capabilities come together. Also the threat of a takeover galvanizes an inefficient firm into action to perform better.

2   Operational synergy is achieved when firms, each below the optimum scale of operations, combine and achieve optimum size. By coming together, economies of scale which arise because of indivisibitities in case of equipment, people and overheads are reaped.

3   Financial synergy also becomes possible. Firms with large internal cash flow and no investment opportunities have excess cash. Firms with low internal generation of funds and large growth opportunities have a need for additional financing. Combination of the two is beneficial. The combined firm's capacity to raise debt can also be greater than the sum of the two firms' capacities before the merger. This provides tax savings on investment income. Because of operational and financial synergy, takeovers lead to a better social allocation of resources.

4   New markets and new capabilities can be developed rather quickly through mergers and takeovers. Entry into new fields is quicker and success is assured by acquiring a firm in that field rather than by making a beginning from the scratch. The increased takeover activity in the USA between 1992 and 1996 was partially motivated by the urge to acquire new skills to augment the firms capacity in relation to new growth areas or to meet new competitive threats.

5   Diversification through mergers and acquisitions is often sought by managers for preserving organizational capital i.e. firm-specific informational assets and for financial and tax advantages.

6   When a tender offer is made to the shareholders of a target firm, its share price goes up and it usually remains high even when the offer turns out to be unsuccessful. So it is hypothesized that a tender offer generates new information and brings about a permanent revaluation of the target firm in the capital market. There are two versions of this information hypothesis. One is that due to the tender offer, the market is informed about the under-valuation of the target firm and this helps in bringing about correct valuation. The target firm does not have to do anything for such a revaluation. This version is known as the "Sitting-on-a-goldmine" version. The other one is that because of the offer, management of the target firm is inspired to implement a more efficient operational strategy. It results, in due course of time, in higher share price. Thus no other outside input but the offer is enough to bring about both higher level of operational efficiency and higher share price.

7 Takeovers serve to minimize agency costs. They are the final weapon for disciplining errant managers. Transaction cost economics states that certain imperfections e.g. indivisibilities, transaction costs, information costs make it inefficient to have labour and capital move individually and separately across firms. Takeovers and mergers may be one means of redeploying corporate resources efficiently across firms while minimizing transaction costs and preserving organizational distinct culture and existence. They are hence a necessary part of a process that is important for maintaining or restoring efficiency.

8 Managers aspire to take over businesses for empire-building, self-fulfillment and job-security motives.

However, the other side of takeovers must also be taken into account. For the following reasons, the potential gains from takeovers may not materialize in reality:

1 In developed countries, it has been consistently found that takeovers proceed in one direction only i.e. larger firms can takeover small firms far more easily rather than the other way round. Thus in a takeover battle, absolute size matters more than relative efficiency.

2 Takeovers lead to short-termism and myopic managerial behaviour. Executives start spending a lot of time on 'road-shows' or presentations to investors and neglect their real work of developing new products, new markets and satisfying consumer needs.

3 Takeover mechanism in the USA has often been used as a device for not honouring the implicit contracts with workers in acquired firms. This discourages the process of firm-specific accumulation of human capital.

4 According to Grossman and Hart, takeovers do not work efficiently because of free-riding problem. An individual shareholder feels that his action is not likely to affect the outcome of a disciplinary takeover bid. So he does not respond to the raider's initial offer but waits until the share price increases. He may keep waiting even after the bid becomes successful. If all shareholders were to act in this fashion, a disciplinary takeover bid will not materialize at all. Small shareholders have an incentive not to tender their shares till the bid fully reflects the impact of higher profitability under new management. However, if the bidder must pay the full price, he cannot gain by acquiring the firm and so he will not make a bid. This results in an impasse.

5 Takeover bids occur when there is ex ante rather than ex post managerial failure. The market for corporate control is a market for contending prospective strategies for firms rather than a mechanism for correcting past poor performance. Also, there does not exist an empirical link between poor firm performance and takeover bids.

6 Takeover bids are typically found to take place in waves while managerial may be perennial/non-perennial but is not cyclical.

7 Costs of takeovers are substantial. There are direct costs in the form of fees to advisers and underwriters and indirect costs in the form of managerial time and effort. These costs have to be borne by the bidder and the target firm. In case of unsuccessful bids, these costs may not necessarily give rise to offsetting benefits.

8 Hostile takeover bids require very high bid premium. So only managerial incompetence in the target firm does not lead to a bid. For it to come forth, the bidder must also foresee other benefits such as strategic gains from a merger. In the USA, almost all corporate bodies have created takeover defenses. They affect shareholder value adversely but serve to protect incumbent management. They have raised bid premia even further.

9 Statutory controls often restrict takeover bids.

10 Free riding problem can also operate like this: after searching extensively to identify businesses with under-utilized resources, a bidder makes a tender offer. Keeping it secret is not possible. The moment a tender offer is made, competitors' attention is attracted to the offer. If competitive bidding starts, the first bidder will lose out because only he has incurred the expense for search and he will have no incentive to undertake any such work in future.

Neo-classical economics sees takeovers as a very health-restoring shake-up process which pinpoints inefficiencies and by removing them reduces slack in the economy. In the myopic market model (See Chapter 4) corporate governance takeovers turn out to be culprits responsible for management's focus on short-term returns to shareholders. Both in the USA and the UK, secondary market has shown sudden spurts of activity for some time, followed by comparative calm for a much longer time. During these short spans takeovers or takeover bids have given a big jolt to complacent managements; have forced them to step up dividend payouts and also to be better at their jobs. Businesses that have been targets of such bids have tried their best to resist them through a number of internal and external defenses.

All in all, takeovers are a costly but sure-fire monitoring mechanism. They are truly a measure of last resort.

Takeovers

Some of the popular takeover defenses used in the USA are explained below.

1. **Dual/multiple-class shares:** Equity shares with different voting rights. Equity stock of a company comprises shares with more than proportional, proportional, less than proportional as well as no voting rights. As has been explained later, fresh issue of such shares is permitted in the USA but *recapitalization* to introduce dual class shares is not permitted.

2. **Poison-pills:** These are securities which entitle their holders to special rights if the issuing company becomes subject to a takeover bid. So bidder's cost of acquiring control without cooperation of incumbent management goes up.

Table 3.1. *Pre-bid defensive response against hostile takeover bids*

Action	Results
Internal Defenses	
1 Improve operational efficiency and reduce costs.	Improved earnings per share (EPS), higher share price and firm value.
2 Improve strategic focus by restructuring, divestment.	Improved EPS, higher firm value. Asset stripping by bidder difficult.
3 Change ownership structure through dual-class shares, high gearing, share buy-back, poison pill*, greenmail* etc.	Control by bidder difficult. Scope for leveraged buyout.
4 Change direction or management structure or incentive structure e.g. staggered board, golden parachute*.	Predator control delayed and bid cost goes up.
5 Cultivate organizational constituencies such as trade unions and workers.	Useful alliances against bidder.
External Defenses	
1 Cultivate shareholders and investors e.g. use investor relations advisor to inform about company performance, prospects and policies.	Ensures loyalty and support of key shareholders.
2 Inform analysts about company strategy, financial policies and investment programmes.	Share under-valuation risk reduced and bid cost goes up.
3 Accept social responsibility to enhance image.	Public hostility to predator aroused.
4 Make strategic defense investment e.g. joint venture/mutual shareholding in fellow targets	Predator control blocked.
5 Monitor the share register for unusual share purchases. Force disclosure of identity of buyers.	Early warning signal about possible predators.

Note: *These terms are explained below.

Typically, a poison pill is put into place by giving a special dividend in the form of a right to purchase additional shares of a particular company's equity. These rights trade like other equity shares until a triggering event takes place. Then the right is detached and it may be exercised at a low price by shareholders other than the bidder. Poison-pills are also referred to as shareholders' rights plans. Within a wide frame of limits set by court decisions, managers have full discretion in determining whether to trigger a poison pill provision.

3. **Greenmail:** It is an agreement in which a company repurchases the stock

Table 3.2. *Post-offer defenses against hostile takeover bids.*

	Defense	Description, Purpose
1	First response and pre-emption letter	Attack bid logic and price. Advise target shareholders not to accept.
2	Defense document	Praise own performance and prospects, deride bid price and logic, form of finance and predator's track record.
3	Profit report/forecast	Report or forecast improved profits for past/current year to make the offer look cheap.
4	Promise high dividend in future	High returns to shareholders weaken predator's promise
5	Asset revaluation	Revalue properties, intangibles and brands, show that bid under-values target.
6	Share support campaign	Enlist own employee pension fund/ESOP. Attempt to block control.
7	Appeal to regulator	Lobby antitrust/regulatory authorities to block bid.
8	Litigation	To enforce antitrust/regulatory rules.
9	Acquisition and divestment	Buy a business to make target look bigger/incompatible with bidder, sell crown jewels to raise bid cost and to throw predator's strategy into disarray.
10	Unions/workers	Enlist support. Lobby politicians.
11	Customers/supplier	Show that relationship with them will be jeopardized.
12	Red herring	Attack predator on peripheral issues.
13	Advertisement	Media campaign to discredit bid.

(Source: PS Sudarsanam, 1997.)

held by a large shareholder, usually at higher than market price, in exchange for the shareholder's agreement not to launch a contest for company control for a specified time period.

4. **Staggered/classified board:** Members of the board are divided into separate classes and are elected to overlapping tenures. Even if there are major upsets in an AGM, the number of directors to be elected gets limited.

5. **Golden parachute:** It is an assurance to executives that if they lose jobs after a takeover, they would be paid compensation.

6. **Blank check preferred stock:** It is authorized preferred stock for which the Board of Directors has broad discretion to establish voting, dividend,

conversion and other rights. It can be used to establish or implement a poison-pill. It is a standby anti-takeover measure.

7. **Stakeholder clause:** By amending the charter or Memorandum of Association of a company, directors are permitted to consider the effects of their decision on other stakeholders such as employees, suppliers, host communities and others. This provides an explicit legal basis to reject takeover bids.

8. **Fair price provision:** It is the price to be paid by a large shareholder and it is typically the highest price paid for any shares acquired earlier. This provision does not apply if the board of directors approves a bid.

9. **Supermajority vote requirement:** For specified actions, a level of approval, set higher than the minimum that is legally specified is set. Typically it is between the range of 75 to 85 per cent of votes cast.

10. **Shareholder meeting requirements:** A restriction on the right to call special shareholder meetings is set. Then shareholders' right to act by written consent is restricted. This right enables shareholders with sufficient votes to take action which otherwise will have to await annual/extraordinary/special general meeting.

11. **Elimination of cumulative voting** or right to alter board size.

12. **Reincorporation to Delaware:** Delaware company law (USA) is friendly to incumbent managers. Many American companies have moved from California which requires cumulative voting and prohibits board classification to Delaware.

The effect of takeover defenses on firm performance and shareholder value has been an important concern. Opposing hypotheses about their relationship are advanced.

Management entrenchment hypothesis argues that takeover defenses push up a bidder's cost of exercising control and they serve to insulate management from market discipline for poor performance. So inefficiency is perpetuated and firm performance goes down. Therefore restrictive takeover defenses reduce managerial diligence and firm performance.

The hypothesis of stockholder interest has two versions. One argues that restrictive takeover defenses reduce the possibility of frivolous or destructive bids. Many takeover bids only serve to divert managers' attention from their core tasks. Takeover threats do not let them take up profitable investment opportunities which are undervalued in financial markets. Takeover defenses, therefore, allow managers to focus on improving business performance in the long run and do indeed, manage to bring about that improvement. (This has overtones of organization-control perspective.)

The other version avers that takeover defenses do not affect internal efficiency or firm performance and have no effect on current profitability of a firm. At the same time, they increase the expected takeover premium and so also the value of the firm. This happens as takeover defenses force bidders to deal with managers rather than individual shareholders. Managers can then negotiate a higher takeover premium than would be possible otherwise. However, firm performance is not affected by takeover defenses.

A study by Karpoff, Marr Danielson (2000) found that firms with takeover defenses as compared to other firms without them in their industries had the best industry-adjusted performance. This study was based on governance profiles of all companies in Standard and Poor 500 index. It pertained to 2 years, 1984 and 1985. It tried to find out effects of individual defense measures. The results were rather ambiguous but it was consistently found that existence of a poison pill was negatively related to firm performance (measured in terms of return on assets and ratio of shares' market and book value). These findings support those of an earlier study – Gordon and Pound, (1991). This study was based on a sample of 1100 American companies and it showed that restrictive governance measures e.g. staggered boards, poison pills, super-majority provisions etc. brought down the company performance over the long run.

Appendix I

History of Voting Rights of Shareholders

In voting, we take 1 share, 1 vote rule for granted today. In India, cooperative societies were promoted as an alternative to capitalist organizations and they adopted 1 person, 1 vote rule. However, corporate businesses have not always followed 1 share, 1 vote rule and a very interesting chapter in business history lies thereby.

If we start tracing the history of corporate firms, we find that till the nineteenth century, 1 share, 1 vote rule was considered almost a sacrilege. State charters to corporate bodies was standard practice and shareholders' rights used to be scrutinized before a charter was granted to a firm. Shareholders mattered as persons and members of a group. Public purpose that a corporation would serve was also important. Statesmen who would debate about grant of charter used to be particular that public purpose of a company did not conflict with the whims of providers of capital. Days of fractioned, diffused public shareholding were of course, far away.

In USA, corporate charters were seen as instruments of abusive power of British kings. Chartered corporations were used by England to maintain control over colonies. So the American corporations that were granted charters were kept under watch by government and citizens. The power to issue corporate charters was retained by the individual states rather than being given to federal government. Many restrictive clauses in these charters ensured that corporations were not used to amass excessive personal power. The early charters used to be for a limited number of years. They also put restrictions on the corporations' borrowings, ownership of land and even profits. Large and small investors had equal voting rights and interlocking directorships were forbidden.

Anglo-American common law safeguarded individuality of shareholders as members of a corporation rather than as owners of a portion of its capital. In 1776, special checks were imposed on powers of large shareholders in order to protect permanent welfare of companies in the USA. Accordingly, voting strength of large shareholders was pegged at some maximum point. In 1781, the Bank of North America's congressional charter generated controversy because it had the 1 share, 1 vote rule in it.

In 1791, Alexander Hamilton, Secretary of the US Treasury, clearly saw the implications of 1 person, 1 vote norm. He stated that the former did not give sufficient importance to large shareholders and put company security in danger. At the same time, the other, 1 share, 1 vote norm, made it easy for large shareholders to come to an agreement and establish their monopoly over the benefits and powers of the corporation. So he suggested a via media in the form of Graduated Voting Rights (GVR).

GVR were to be so designed as to give full representation to small shareholders but limit the voting rights of large shareholders according to a fixed scale. Thus power of capital would be curbed to some extent and a degree of democracy would be achieved in company affairs. Unchecked power, whether possessed by landlords, family dynasties or even governments had always given rise to fear and suspicion in the US and Hamilton was echoing popular sentiment.

GVR were popular in the US around the turn of the eighteenth century. The South Carolina Railroad Company, incorporated in 1827, had the following GVR with 11 scales:

South Carolina Railroad Company 1828

Number of shares owned	Number of votes
1, 2	1
3, 4	2
5, 6	3
7, 8	4
9, 10, 11	5
12, 13, 14, 15	6
16 to 20	7
21 to 26	8
27 to 33	9
34 to 40	10
For every 10 shares in excess of 40	1

Out of 61 charters granted by the South Carolina legislature between 1825 and 1838, only 5 pertaining to smaller companies had 1 share, 1 vote rule. In 1829, the Massachusetts legislature granted 4 railway charters of which 3 had GVR. In Virginia, all manufacturing companies had to adhere to a flat voting scale as per a law passed in 1836. In 1848, another law specified the following voting scale:

For every share from 1 to 20   —   1 vote
For every 2 shares from 21 to 200   —   1 vote
For every 5 shares from 201 to 500   —   1 vote
For every 10 shares above 500   —   1 vote

Till 1840, GVR were widespread in the US. Only New York was an exception, having granted incorporation to manufacturing companies with 1 share, 1 vote rule right since 1811. In 1850, a general railroad law was passed which endorsed the above norm. After this law the GVR system started declining. The last corporate charter with a ceiling on large shareholders' voting rights (at 1/10th of the total votes) was granted in Connecticut in 1841. Between 1850 and 1880, 1 share, 1 vote gradually became the general practice. Only Massachusetts held out till 1880. Thereafter, this traditional guard against concentration of economic power lapsed. (Ironically at the same time, in the political arena in the USA there was a sustained move towards more democratic methods for avoiding concentration of power.)

In Europe, as in the US, corporate practice on voting was mixed but, 1 person 1 vote norm clearly enjoyed popularity, particularly in continental Europe. In Britain too, the charter of the Great Western Railway in 1835 had GVR which operated as:

For holding up to 20 shares — 1 share, 1 vote

For holding shares in excess of 20 — for every 5 shares, 1 additional vote.

Both GVR and the common law rule of 1 person, 1 vote were popular in Europe till the end of the nineteenth century. In Britain, the Companies Act, 1862 carried the famous *Table A* which provided model provisions for Articles of Association of incorporated companies. It had a graduated scale for voting rights. It allotted 1 vote per share for the first 10 shares and thereafter voting rights were proportionally reduced for larger holdings. *Table A* was mandatory for unlimited and limited-by-guarantee companies and it applied to limited companies, limited by shares if their own articles were silent on voting rights. A new *Table A* which recognized 1 share, 1 vote was published in 1906 but graduated scales were in use till 1916.

In France, corporate charters often specified lower threshold in share ownership and an upper threshold on the number of votes a shareholder could cast. GVR were widely used among Prussian railroads and banks around 1850. The Prussian-Rhenish Railroad Charter in 1836 had voting rights with 14 graduations. There were other similar examples. The Company law in Germany was substantially revised in 1884. While giving every shareholder a right to vote and while recognizing 1 share, 1 vote rule, it also gave an option to companies to limit shareholders' voting rights in various ways. And indeed, companies actually continued to cap large shareholders' voting rights in order to avoid concentration of power in their hands.

The big difference between Europe and the US, in the nineteenth century was that smaller shareholders were often denied voting rights in Europe whereas in the US every shareholder, no matter how small, had a right to vote. European companies favoured 1 person, 1 vote rule while in US, as explained above, 1 share, 1 vote rule had gained general acceptance by 1900. After taking these opposite tendencies into account, historians have concluded that European companies were more democratic and American companies plutocratic. Robert Liefmann, a German authority on cartels and trusts, noted with surprise at the beginning of the twentieth century that American companies were much less democratically governed as compared to their German counterparts.

Plutocracy in America did not mean dominance of large shareholders in reality. By the middle nineteenth century itself, corporate firms had reached a critical point in their activities: they needed large capital to expand the scale of operations and their internal, administrative complexities were such that managerial input had become a key factor in their working. Share capital had to be collected from general public. So widely distributed shareholding and strong executives were required. As explained earlier, this created a pattern of weak shareholders and strong managers.

Appendix II

Shareholders' Voting Rights in the USA in the Twentieth Century

Between 1920 and 1925, voting rights of shareholders were again in limelight in the USA. Public utility companies had issued substantial non-voting shares and because of them, executives owning few shares had managed to establish personal control over these companies. In one of them – Industrial Rayon – 6,00,000 equity shares carrying only 2,000 votes had been issued. Abuse of their extraordinary power by executives began immediately and the whole industry was brought to a point of virtual collapse. People lost their confidence in the capital market and inflow of funds for investment began drying up. Public sentiment was aroused against controlling shareholders. So the Public Utility Holding Company Act, 1935 had to be passed.

In 1940s, a similar situation arose in the investment industry in the USA. This industry had become very popular and it was found that 1 out of every 10 investors held shares of investment companies. Entrepreneurs responded to this uncommon enthusiasm of investors by issuing multiple classes of shares with divergent voting rights. These led to a good deal of corruption and abuse. So the Investment Companies Act, 1940 came to be passed. Section 18 of this Act made 1 share, 1 vote norm mandatory for investment companies.

After a lull of 40-odd years, the issue of voting rights became important once again during the takeover era of the 1980s. When the spectre of hostile takeover bids started haunting managers, they thought of protecting themselves by taking away the voting rights of at least some types of shareholders. New shares without voting rights were offered to shareholders at heavy discounts in exchange for old shares with voting rights. Discounts and other incentives were so attractive that individual shareholders found it impossible to refuse these offers which collectively made all shareholders less powerful.

Fears of an active role by institutional investors and prospects of real accountability drove managements to continue to offer shares with less than 1 vote per share. This move amounted to making their companies private without having to pay the full price in terms of restricted access to capital. The dual or multiple class system of shares soon became a deluge. In this system, 1 class of shares has disproportionately high voting rights while another class comprises only non-voting shares. In the past, dual shares structure was used in the USA only in a few, traditionally family-run companies. Now every one wanted capital from public but keep control private. Interestingly, many stock exchanges also amended their listing rules and allowed companies to issue these shares. In 1986, New York Stock Exchange, a strong adherent to 1 share, 1 vote rule right since 1811, asked Securities Exchange Commission (SEC) for its permission to drop this rule as it feared flight of capital to other states and a reduction in its licensing fees.

The New York Stock Exchange (NYSE) wanted to allow the issue of multiple class equity provided a majority of independent directors and public shareholders of the company approved this action. The SEC initially deferred action, hoping that the American Stock Exchange (AMEX), NASDAQ and NYSE would sort out the issue among themselves. When they failed to do so, the SEC was forced to take a stand on this issue.

The stated justification for recapitalization schemes was that centralizing control in the hands of those with superior voting rights would increase firm value and also the value of limited voting rights shares. So enhanced dividend or higher price in future would compensate for the loss of voting rights. Critics of dual-class recapitalizations compared this move with LBOs. (In a Leveraged Buy-out [LBO], a bank or investment fund acquiring a company, replaces the latter's equity with various forms of debt. Business operations are carried out by using the debt capacity of the firm. After 3 to 5 years, the firm is sold or floated again on the stock exchange with substantial capital gain for the bank/fund. 'Cash cows' or companies with steady cash flow, mature products and readily disposable assets are prime targets of LBO.) Shareholders of a company subject to LBO, receive a substantial premium while in recapitalization, shareholders whose voting rights are to be reduced, receive only a small dividend hike for surrendering control. So recapitalizations were thought to be against the interest of shareholders. It was indeed true that in all the recapitalization schemes, finally management or/and existing dominant shareholding group had come to possess an equity block with greater voting strength while voting strength of public or outside shareholders was reduced.

In the debate that followed, one side pressed the SEC to allow dual or multiple class recapitalizations in the interest of efficient self-selection. Let one more option to design capital structure be there for business; each firm would choose what is best for itself, was the argument. The other side wanted recapitalization to be banned as it was coercive and went against the interest of particularly small shareholders. Empirical evidence was not sufficient to settle the matter. It showed that LBOs were useful in case of successful companies with large market shares in mature, slow-growth industries while entrepreneurial companies in high-growth industries preferred recapitalization schemes so as not to dilute control.

It was argued before the SEC that coercion could be said to exist only if the dominant shareholder group's position was strengthened *at the expense* of existing public shareholders. A rule that allowed public offering of a new class of low or non-voting shares could allow new equity to be raised without abridging the rights of existing shareholders. Such an offer would not be coercive. Thus prohibiting the alteration of voting rights of existing public shareholders but *not* the sale of a second class of limited or non-voting equity would precisely thread the way between efficient self-selection and coercion.

Indeed, the SEC accepted this logic. Therefore dual-class capital structures remain valid but dual-class recapitalizations are banned. This is where matters rest now.

This section has covered only some of the prominent developments as regards voting rights of shareholders. However, they are enough for us to appreciate that voting rights play a fundamental role in corporate governance. The overriding lesson that can be drawn from these developments is that separation of ownership from voting rights increases agency costs which add to inefficiencies in corporate oversight.

4

Perspectives and Models of Corporate Governance

Three Perspectives

Three distinct perspectives on corporate governance can be discerned in the existing literature. Each perspective is a way of approaching the issues related to governance of corporate bodies and of deciding the right solutions. These perspectives are:
1 Shareholder – or capital market – control perspective
2 Organization – or management – control perspective
3 Stakeholder – control perspective
Differences in these perspectives are summarized in the following table:
According to the first perspective, shareholders as providers of risk capitals, have final control over resource allocation decision. However, in reality, managers take this control away and their self-interest leads them to pursue growth rather than profits. Instead of returning free cash flow to shareholders, managers invest it in avenues which are not the most profitable ones and then sloth sets in. To prevent the resultant decline in company performance, stock market must enable shareholders to loosen managers' control over excess funds. This will serve to limit managers' power and to achieve greater efficiency in resource allocation in the corporate economy.

Organization-control perspective believes that managers who coordinate the efforts of different factors of production and who contribute their skill and creativity to the production process are primarily responsible for generating surplus. They invest in R & D and organizational learning and they locate new markets. Their specialized grasp of operational matters and their professionalism are of vital importance. It is they who create profitable opportunities to add value. Therefore resource allocation decision should rest with them.

Stakeholder-control perspective is a new perspective. It argues that not shareholder-value maximization but well-being of all groups with a stake in the

Table 4.1. *Different perspectives of governance*

Particular	Shareholder-control perspective	Organization-control perspective	Stakeholder-control
1 Critical resource or source of value	Portfolio investors	Production process, organizational learning, locating new markets	Human capital
2 Controlling authority	Shareholders	Managers	Employees with firm-specific investment
3 Governance problem	Managerial opportunism	Tyranny of financial markets leading to short-termism	No representation to employees in resource-allocation decisions
4 Solution	Block holders-individual or institutional becoming active owners, takeovers	Relational investment, measures to make shareholder exit more costly	Board of Directors with representation of employees, possibly other stake-holders

long-run success of a business should be the goal of corporate governance. This is not meant to be just a normative prescription. This approach is expected to result in long-term sustenance and efficiency of business. For example, it is shown that firms which enjoy a reputation for ethical dealings with customers, suppliers and employees, are able to build up trust-based relationships which support profitable investments. By citing cases of Germany and Japan, an attempt is made to show that stakeholder involvement leads to long-term value maximization while simultaneously avoiding agency problem. It is also argued that neglect of other stakeholders — particularly employees — leads to under-investment in human-skills. This is detrimental to the interest of the organization. The German firms solve this problem through co-determination while the Japanese firms use life-time employment and consensus-based decision-making for the purpose. The American and the British firms do not have similar beneficial mechanisms and so their labour productivity has continued to fall behind.

Organization-control perspective was seen mainly in the USA till recently and the controversy about corporate governance in that country is essentially a tussle between it and the shareholder-control perspective. The rest of the world is dominated by shareholder-control perspective. In the UK it takes the form of capital-market control while in Germany and Japan, block holders (majority shareholders) control companies.

To understand shareholder-control perspective better, we have to distinguish between two types of shareholders viz. owner-investors and portfolio investors. Owner-investors are interested in the business i.e. its wealth and profit-making capacity over a period of time. They are serious about their ownership responsibilities and have a longer time frame as compared to portfolio investors. The latter use the capital market to build up their asset portfolio and by shuffling its contents as per market trends, try to maximize returns.

It can be seen that with a developed capital market, active owners are generally passive investors and active investors are passive owners. Owner-investors and portfolio investors follow different strategies. Owner investors provide dedicated capital while portfolio investors use the capital market to buy and sell shares continuously. Capital-market control perspective refers to portfolio investors and to the dominance of stock price as the foremost indicator of corporate performance. If a small shareholder wants to take his ownership seriously and if he keeps his shares with himself for a long time, it does not mean anything. Collective action problem is too severe to make this a meaningful choice. On the other hand, block holders – individual/family/institutional shareholders – might go for relationship investment. Thus we have to make a fine distinction between shareholder-control perspective and capital market perspective. The former might mean relationship investment by block holders and the latter – control by capital market on behalf of portfolio investors. In short, the moment we distinguish between owner-investors and portfolio investors, we also have to distinguish between shareholder-control and capital market-control perspectives. Shareholder-control perspective looks at corporate governance from the point of view of block holders while capital market-control perspective does so from the viewpoint of portfolio investors.

Shareholder-control perspective in this sense and organization-control perspective are not necessarily antagonistic. Some block holders and managers can come together to bring about sustained organizational progress. This is frequently seen in Germany, Japan and also, to some extent, in India. Capital market-control perspective and organization-control perspective are however, in the opposite camps. Organization-control perspective came under fire in the USA because of executive excesses and because of executive failure to maximize shareholder-value. Supporters of organization-control perspective hit back by pointing to short-termism i.e. neglect of long-run corporate sustainability by companies in order to engineer short-run gains in stock prices. This short-termism continues to be the main point of criticism against capital market-control perspective.

Both shareholder and organization-control perspectives are based on the theory of managerialism, originally formulated by Berle and Means (1932). Managerialism argues that in large industrial corporations which enjoy considerable freedom in the product market due to their big size, scattered and absentee shareholding has created a power vacuum which is filled by managers. It states further that efforts by shareholders to limit managerial exuberance are largely ineffective. However, the most important point in this formulation is about product market freedom. If a competitive product market keeps the players on their toes constantly, room for managerial self-aggrandizement is automatically reduced.

However, there is a crucial difference between the two perspectives as regards managerialism. Shareholder-control perspective concentrates on managerial opportunism and diversion of interest between managers and shareholders. Organization-control perspective stresses the positive aspects of managerial control which follow from their emphasis on organizational well-being.

There are pointers that managers have never enjoyed total or absolute control except in some cases in the USA and there too, the situation has changed radically in the last two decades. In large corporate bodies in the USA, non-executive directors dominate the board and many of them have significant shareholding in their companies. In the UK, institutional investors form the largest group of shareholders today. Both these groups – non-executive directors and institutional investors – have started taking greater interest in governance of companies following the developments since 1980s and also because of the exhortations of various committees on corporate governance. Therefore, there is limited empirical support to managerialism.

With various instances of executive excesses, frauds and corporate failures, when the issue of corporate governance burst upon the scene in the USA, powerlessness of shareholders and elimination of organizational slack by takeovers were the initial prominent issues. It was thought that growing clout of institutional investors would be an effective remedy to the problem. Growing competition in product markets and changes in consumer demand which undermined markets of large firms added to the attack on organization-control perspective. Its bureaucratic view of business and its underestimation of the power of capital market were felt to belong to a bygone era and these gave a measure of poignancy to the debate.

Although the debate roundly castigated managers for their lack of account-ability to shareholders, it must be mentioned in retrospect that these managers had retained earnings and invested them to make their organizations strong. Because of their investment in organizational innovation, their firms had remained on top in the market and had grown continuously. In handing over control to shareholders, many an executive feared that short-run considerations would prevail over long-run sustenance of firms and these firms would start regressing.

The classical view of corporate governance emphasized the satisfaction of outside financiers to ensure that supply of external funds to business did not dry up. Stakeholder-control perspective argues that it is no longer necessary to couch the issue exclusively in favour of financiers because finance has ceased to be the key input in running businesses. Along with capital, physical assets, brand names, government licenses etc. also no longer give differential advantage to any firm. Innovation has become the most crucial factor and this has increased the importance of human resources. This can be seen not only in high technology sectors but also in banking, advertising and many service industries.

In the last two decades, vertically integrated large firms have been under attack because of active, mobile capital flows across the globe and rapid changes in consumer demand. These firms have been forced to subcontract their work or to relocate to places which have cheap labour. After the phase of downsizing and delayering is over, specialized teams of knowledge-workers have become important in them. In short, human capital is now the key resource in many firms.

At the same time, rate of turnover of human capital has increased. More opportunities are available in the market for both wage and self-employment and so employees today tend to change jobs more often. Therefore the priority in corporate governance is not monitoring top managers but retaining employees and keeping them motivated. For this purpose it is necessary to create complementarities or links that cause individuals to be better off voluntarily following the firm's commands rather than acting on their own. Long-term stock options, granting privileged access to critical resources to employees who have firm-specific specialization are likely to be the required corrective measures.

Rising importance of human capital has also meant the weakening of command and control system within firms. Surplus is not concentrated at the top but is shared evenly throughout the enterprise. Enterprises in the new technology sectors do not require massive investment. So ownership and operational control are once again coming together. As per stakeholder-control perspective, governance has to move beyond monitoring of top managers and beyond ensuring their accountability to financiers.

Another strand of stakeholder perspective argues that any corporate body will be run most effectively if all stakeholders have appropriate levels of empowerment and if managers recognize their accountability to all stakeholders. Control of executive power is important in any governance mechanism. Similar to the famous division among judiciary, legislature and executive in the American constitution, division of power at the top is required in any organization – the bigger it is, the more pressing the need. Downsizing of the 1980s and the 1990s has resulted in a tendency for untrammelled autocracy among managers. They have also pursued short-term dividends/share-price gains to the exclusion of every other objective. So limiting executive exuberance is absolutely essential. Inclusion of non-executive directors representing stakeholders other than shareholders is therefore necessary. Provision of dedicated capital and grant of restricted stock options to employees in lieu of a part of their wages are also desirable. These reforms in corporate governance will have to be carried out through institutional arrangements and statutory edicts. Capital market will not be of any use for this purpose as it looks only at short-run availability of financial capital.

Stakeholder-control perspective is generally ignored. Its critics point out that in trying to implement it, managers will lose focus, decisiveness and they will also be able to rationalize any action by citing some alleged benefits for some stakeholders. The outcome would certainly be more managerial autonomy to pursue private benefits of control. Secondly, managers would consider the welfare of only stakeholders with power and they would form an alliance with them to expropriate other stakeholders. Simultaneously, managers would try to influence regulation to promote ideas of a stakeholder society to gain more autonomy.

Thus the above three perspectives have different foci and they suggest different remedial measures. The difference among them can be brought out with respect to Employees Stock Option Plans (ESOPs). Organization-control perspective has an ambivalent stand on this issue. On one hand, it is thought that they will make managers think and act like owners and thus agency problem will be addressed. On the other hand, the possibility that they will result in a short-term, stock market orientation of executive decisions cannot be denied. Hence they would exacerbate short-termist pressure unless suitable steps by way of restrictions on these options are taken. Shareholder-control perspective is against ESOPs. It is thought that they will lead to further entrenchment of managers whose remuneration would rise by option gains if share prices go up and by the usual route of salary, perks and commission if they do not. Further, corporate governance system would head for a breakdown as separation between managers and owners would get blurred. Capital market-control perspective is unambiguously in favour of ESOPs. Stakeholder-control perspective believes that stock options are essential not only for managers and employees but also for all other stakeholders too, in order to forge a community of interest in governance.

The difference in these perspectives can be seen with reference to the role of capital market also. Organization-control perspective believes that threat of takeovers and recourse to high dividend payout to avoid them has been responsible for diverting managers' attention from organizational investment and learning in the long run. It attributes declining competitive position of the American industry to this short-termism (See 61p) induced by the capital market. Capital market-control perspective on the other hand, concentrates on agency costs and the divergence of interest between shareholders and managers. It lauds the role of capital market in forcing managers to part with excess surplus and to hand it over to shareholders.

As per capital market-control perspective, corporate governance reforms should concentrate on strengthening investor rights and the capital market. A liquid capital market enables shareholders to make their exit quietly and painlessly from unprofitable investments. Similarly the secondary capital market keeps managers on their toes and ensures that sloth and resource wastage do not take place.

Organization-control perspective, on the other hand, argues that corporate governance reforms should concentrate on creating an environment in which managers and shareholders are encouraged to share long-term performance horizons. Specifically, relational investment, restrictions on takeovers, inducement for shareholder loyalty and empowerment of other stakeholders are advocated. As per market-control perspective, these reforms would be counter-productive as cost of shareholder exit would go up and they would become more vulnerable to managerial opportunism.

Stakeholder-control perspective makes a case for representation of stakeholders – particularly employees – at the board level, granting them stock options etc.

[**Short-termism** occurs when a firm applies an excessive discount rate or a fore-shortened time horizon to its investment projects. This creates a tilt in favour of projects with short-term payback periods and investment in research and development, employee training etc. is reduced as these are long-term investments with uncertain returns.

The stock market is supposed to have ushered in short-termism in the UK and the USA but many analysts point their finger at corporate managers for strengthening this bias. Thus causes of short-termism can be both *external* and *internal* to a firm. The former include: objectives of institutional investors, their performance criteria for fund managers, treatment of different types of investment in accounting standards, managers' perception of capital market, its efficiency etc. Internal factors cover performance evaluation measures and remuneration of top managers. Particularly the inclusion of stock market-based performance – linked components in managerial pay is believed to be a major internal factor.

It is argued that short-termism distorts decision-making by not allowing due consideration to be given to the long-term and that it creates difficulties in international competition since Germany and Japan have not yet been afflicted by this malady. At the same time, short-termism is believed to be beneficial in reducing corporate slack.]

Important Questions

With such diverse approaches to the problem and its solutions, the whole issue of corporate governance has become highly complex. Finally, any perspective on corporate governance has to finally answer the following important questions:

1 Can shareholders become involved in monitoring managers while simultaneously using a liquid stock market and maintaining their independence of judgement?
2 What should be the role of hostile takeover bids?
3 Should attention be focused only on the impact of corporate actions on shareholders or should corporate governance include the larger social impact of these actions?

4   What is the nature of shareholders' ownership claim? Can restrictions be placed over their contractual freedom to maximize returns?
5   Is corporate governance debate concerned only with efficient use of resources or with distributional issues – for example, transfer of surplus from firms to shareholders, employees, other stakeholders and implications of this transfer – as well?

Theory of Corporate Governance

The study of corporate structure dates back to Berle and Means (1932), Alfred Marshall (1920) and Adam Smith (1716) in reverse chronological order. These writers focused on the separation between ownership and control in the corporate form. Adam Smith expressed doubts about the efficiency of managers and directors in managing foreign ventures. He felt that they managed other peoples' money and so were negligent with it. Therefore joint stock companies for foreign trade were not able to compete successfully with private adventurers. According to Marshall, self-interest led salaried managers to adopt a policy of least resistance. So he did not try hard to improve matters, nor did he adopt improvements suggested by others till their success was proved beyond doubt.

Berle and Means thought that widely scattered, small shareholdings of corporations would progressively leave more power in the hands of managers as individual shareholders would have little incentive to monitor and control the affairs of the firm. At the same time, managers' ownership rights in large firms were too small to make them interested in profit maximization. So appropriate monitoring devices had to be fashioned. James Burnham (1941) also made an early discussion of the impact of professional managers on corporate direction.

Cyert and March (1963) argued that corporate executives had to satisfy many groups and individuals through decision-making and hence the corporation was concerned with 'satisficing' rather than profit maximization. Marris (1964) stated that shareholders were interested in maximizing return on their investment while managers might well be interested in maximizing growth and personal security. Power, status, opportunity for creative satisfaction and group-belonging could be other motives of managers. From this rather simple, plausible probability, Marris hypothesized that a takeover threat was a major constraint on the growth of a corporate firm. His line of reasoning was: when a firm's valuation ratio (market value divided by book value of stock) fell below what was considered to be its real value by a potential bidder, a takeover struggle would begin. To avoid it, existing management would have to give high dividend so as to maintain a high market value of stock. The resultant short-term orientation in managerial decision-making would conflict with long-term value maximization. Such a behaviour has become a major criticism of Anglo-American corporate governance today.

Another strand of thinking on corporate bodies notes the strain between owners and managers and goes on to enquire whether a mechanism to do right by workers, suppliers, customers while simultaneously serving public interest can be created Mason (1958). ECB Gower (1969), lamented that workers formed an integral part of a company but company law ignored this reality. Robert Dahl (1970), an advocate of the view that a firm functioned on the basis of its implicit contract with society, he stated that interest group management was the main task of the board of directors and accordingly directorships ought to be apportioned among important constituencies. Thus one-third of the board seats should go to employees' representatives, one-third to consumers and one-third to government representatives. But Dahl does not mention any shareholder representation on the board. C Summers (1982) and Masahiko Aoki (1983) take up Gower's view and asserts that employees, who work far more for a corporate firm as compared to its shareholders ought to have greater say in corporate governance. The stakeholder perspective of corporate governance, as stated above, incorporates these insights and builds upon them.

Insights from Transaction Cost Economics
Transaction Cost Economics (TCE) is closely associated with the study of industrial organizations because it posits that firms emerge as a result of the need to reduce transaction costs. These costs are costs of measuring what is exchanged and of enforcing agreements. They are the costs of using price mechanism or the economic equivalent of friction in physical mechanisms.

For attaining economies in transaction costs, different institutions or governance structures must be compared. They vary from the classical perfect market at one end to a centralized, hierarchical organization at the other, with several mixed forms in between. (In a perfectly competitive market, a homogeneous product is sold to all buyers at a constant price while a hierarchy may be the sole buyer and it may negotiate and contract separately for everything that it buys. In between, there exist bilateral agreements and more complex forms of contracting.) TCE concentrates on the following as the main governance mechanisms:

a   Board of Directors
b   Takeovers
c   Block holding or relational investment.

Board of Directors is an internal (to a firm) mechanism and the other two, being external, can be seen as contending arrangements.

Williamson (1985) zeroes in on the board as a governance structure that is created as a safeguard between the firm and shareholders on the one hand and the firm and management on the other. He sees it as a discretionary control instrument that is efficiently awarded to residual claimants viz. equity-holders in firms in which investments in durable, non-redeployable physical assets are significant. So the refusal to award control over the board in such firms to equity finance poses an investment hazard, the effect of which is to raise the price of finance. Williamson wonders if membership of the board can be open to members of constituencies other than shareholders. Two types of board membership are considered viz. informational and voting membership. The former serves to secure information only while voting membership goes with authority to ratify management decisions and monitor its performance. Williamson's conclusion is that informational board membership may be selectively offered to other constituencies but anything more would involve trade-offs with *doubtful net benefits*. He states that, "Most constituencies are better advised to perfect their relation to the firm at the contracting interface at which firm and constituencies strike their main bargain."

Specifically in case of labour, Williamson's argument is that employees with only general purpose skills and knowledge do not deserve board membership as they can be easily replaced. Employees with firm-specific skills should be given higher wages or informational participation on the board so as to create a governance structure that will safeguard this asset. Claude Menard (1997) has therefore formulated a general principle regarding board membership: only those constituents holding highly specific assets and not in a position to obtain ex ante guarantees that could protect them against opportunism, will systematically seek significant power in the government of formal organizations.

In relational investment, large shareholders provide long-term or 'patient' capital. They can have a seat on the board and they can participate in policy-making and in monitoring management directly. Still, it is a very intrusive form of governance.

All firms do not need block holders and all large shareholders do not need to be relational investors. Again, there are two varieties of relational investing: in the soft type, a block holder intervenes only during crises but is passive otherwise. In the strong variety, the block holder has a seat on the board and he participates in monitoring. This strong variety will be seen only in firms with:

1   most of their assets in non-redeployable form i.e. intangible assets or tangible assets which are highly specialized in a particular line of activity
2   uncertain cash-flows from these assets; these are new firms whose capacity to develop not known the value of their assets is known or firms that have volatile customer demand of technological needs.

In these firms, it is necessary to closely monitor management and to have timely access to information. Otherwise equity could be squandered away without ready detection in the market. So the block holder does not allow outside directors to mediate between management and shareholders; he does the job himself.

Insights from Contract Theory
Contract theory begins by arguing that to solve the agency problem (i.e. the problem of divergence of interest between principal and agent. See principal-agent model, 65p), it would be sufficient to write a contract specifying what managers should do with investors' funds and how they should distribute the returns between themselves and investors. Ideally, this contract should foresee every problem that might arise in the manager's task of using funds, earning

returns and allocating them. Such contracts are however, not feasible as there is no way to foresee all the problems that might arise in future. So these contracts, if attempted, will necessarily remain incomplete. The important question that then arises is: in circumstances not specified in the contract, who should have control rights? These could be called residual control rights. They should vest in investors. Every time something unforeseen happens, managers should refer the concerned matter to investors. In practice, this does not work as investors themselves do not know what to do. So managers end up with substantial residual control rights. They turn out to be even more substantial in reality because of the following two problems:

1 If interpretation and verification of contracts between investors and managers were to be left with independent courts, managers' discretion would be reduced. But normally courts do not interfere in cases that can be clubbed under *business judgement rule* and confine themselves only to the more flagrant cases of violation of investors' rights.

2 Investors, particularly small investors face the problem of collective action.

So managers enjoy large discretionary power and the result is managerial opportunism ranging from the crudest instance of walking away with investors' money to more subtle forms such as transfer pricing, selling firm's output to a manager's own business at less than market price, selling firm's assets the same way, getting excessive perquisites, undertaking pet projects that do not benefit shareholders and finally hanging on to their job long past their utility.

In short, writing a contract does not solve the problem of agency. Perhaps an incentive contract for managers would do the trick. Profit-based commission and stock options on the one hand and threat of dismissal should the firm's income or profit fall below a certain point on the other, might be effective. However, empirical evidence shows low correlation between executive pay and firm performance. Therefore even incentive contracts fail to solve the agency problem adequately.

Models of Corporate Governance

Principal-Agent Model: (Hart, Jensen, Meckling)
Capital market-control perspective of corporate governance is based on this model. Shareholders are principals who provide their funds for carrying on business and managers who are the paid employees, are their agents. There is no guarantee that managers will strive for maximizing shareholder value.

Separation of ownership from control gives rise to agency problem. It brings agency costs into existence. They include:
- cost of structuring contracts between owners and managers
- cost of monitoring managers
- bonding cost to ensure that agent makes optimal decisions or that principal is compensated for any sub-optimal decision made by the agent.

According to Jensen and Meckling, an agency problem arises when managers own only a fraction of the total shares issued by a company. This partial ownership causes them to work less vigorously than otherwise or to consume more perquisites because majority owners will bear most of the cost.

Another form of this model posits that a business promoter recognizes that managers can deviate from the goal of maximum shareholder value and so he imposes rules to regulate their conduct. He appoints auditors when he invites external equity. These rules and provision of auditing are essential to attract external equity. As ownership becomes more diffuse, managers work less hard and firm value declines. At the same time, constraint of funds goes away. Soon, the way is paved for professionalization of management. The benefits of wealth diversification and professionalization outweigh the decline in firm value caused by agency costs. Hence external equity will be sought. It will be brought in till a point of equality between costs and benefits is reached. Capital structure of a firm will reflect such an equilibrium reached as a result of bargaining freely carried out by owners and outside investors. Therefore any external intervention will only serve to distort matters.

This model recognizes that agency costs that must be incurred to bring managers' working in line with shareholder interest, present costs to the economic system. However, their existence leads to innovations in governance such as employee stock options, leveraged buy-outs etc.

Internal regulation of manager's conduct, appointment of independent auditors, inclusion of non-executive directors in Board of Directors are important internal corporate governance mechanisms. An individual shareholder is given an extremely limited voice in this arrangement. This is so in spite of the right to vote that rests with ordinary shareholders as residual claimants. To exercise their voting right effectively, shareholders will have to congregate and that will be a costly arrangement. Also such an assembly generally works under special circumstances only and not as a regular arrangement. On the other hand, access to liquid stock markets gives the shareholders unrestricted, low-cost, exit option. Particularly the market for corporate control plays a very important role in this model. It is presumed to generate large benefits for shareholders in the process of moving resources to their highest valued use. Such a movement of funds keeps corporations agile and guarantees their viability. These elements – internal arrangement, residual voting rights of shareholders, product and capital markets – represent governance mechanisms which ultimately commit corporate resources to value-maximizing ends. It is believed that in the crises of the early 1990s, the internal governance mechanism in companies in the USA and the UK failed but the external mechanism represented by the secondary capital market worked well. If additional obligations are imposed on the corporate boards in the interest of employees as stakeholders., then owners of business will simply stop taking in external equity. Hence corporate governance reforms will have to take the form of, at the most, voluntary efforts to implement a code of best practices.

Several indications of the severity of agency problem are available. Whenever a takeover bid is announced, share price of the target firm jumps up. Bidders generally end up with substantial profits for themselves. Incumbent managers resist takeovers for protecting their private benefits of control. Jensen found that in the oil industry, free cash flow was reinvested in spite of poor investment opportunities but it was not returned to shareholders.

Criticism of Principal-Agent Model

This model assumes that whenever agents substitute their own objectives for those of their principals, business performance becomes inferior as agents divert and waste resources and get themselves entrenched. However, these are not the only outcomes possible. In many corporations, agents built strong, forward-looking organizations which brought unprecedented prosperity to the USA after the Second World War. So it must not be forgotten that managerial effort adds value and that shareholders' interference in management will probably reduce firm value.

Agency problem or the conflict between shareholders and managers was the crux of the corporate governance problem in the USA. In other corporate governance systems and in India, conflict between inside and outside shareholders or between block holders and minority shareholders takes its place. In fact, collusion between inside shareholders and managers and expropriation of minority interest is the main governance problem the world over.

Charkham has criticized agency model's assumption regarding human behaviour viz. only self-interest motivates people and carrot-and-stick approach is necessary to keep them on their toes. Secondly, he points out that managerial competence rather than motivation should be focused on in this discussion as many businesses are ruined by incompetence rather than wrong motives. The main purpose of creating accountability, according to him should be to maintain standards of competence.

Myopic Market Model

It was Marris who first stated that a takeover threat was a major constraint on the growth of an enterprise. He reasoned that managers would have to declare high dividends and maintain high stock prices to avoid takeover bids. The resultant bias in their decisions for the short-run would conflict with maximization of long-term shareholder value.

An excessive concern for short-term returns has become an important point of criticism of capital market-control perspective and the Anglo-American corporate governance system today. It is observed that capital market systematically undervalues long-term capital investment by corporations. It forces managers to judge their actions only on the basis of their effect on share price or else face a hostile takeover. However, according to this model, share price is not always a useful indicator of firm value and the capital market is not always an efficient selection mechanism. In its view, a takeover threat becomes simply a distraction from the true task of creating long-term competitive advantage for the firm. Some analysts argue that takeovers are a symptom of a major defect in the working of free markets: a quick takeover cannot act as a substitute for the arduous, painstaking and slow work of internal growth. Internal growth requires careful planning, training of personnel, product development, innovative marketing strategies, building relationships with suppliers etc. In contrast, an acquisition can be accompanied in a matter of months or weeks. Takeovers typically have a clustering tendency and then they taper off.

Myopic market model can thus be seen to support organization-control perspective. The objective of corporate governance reform, according to it, is to create an environment in which managers and shareholders are encouraged to share long-term performance horizons. So relational investment, restrictions on voting rights for short-term or portfolio shareholders, empowerment of groups that have a long-term relationship with a firm and restrictions on takeovers are advocated. Porter (1992) argues for investment incentives to companies for employee training and R & D, expansion of public disclosures, disclosure of information to large, long-term owners under rules that bar trading on it, board representation to customers and suppliers etc.

Political Economy Model (Hellwig)

This model looks at corporate governance as a system of two parts comprising inside and outside stakeholders. Alternately, insiders are supposed to make up the corporate governance system and outsiders – political system. (Roe [1994] makes a distinction between production system or colloquially, Main Street and financial system or Wall Street.)

Individual players in the system are shown in the diagram below.

The distinction between insiders and outsiders is crucial in the working of the system. There is informal, discreet give-and-take between managers and other stakeholders. By exchanging favours, managers regularly find allies in the political system, the media, trade unions, judiciary etc. and they cultivate these allies.

The two systems – corporate governance and political – are linked together because of this exchange of favours. The insiders provide each other with mutual control as well as protection against interference from outsiders. Among them, managers are the most powerful insiders as they have control over corporate resources. Managers' main objective is to insulate themselves from outsiders in order to retain their autonomy. For this purpose, they influence policies to encourage dispersion of ownership and take steps to disenfranchise outside shareholders. Their ability to enlist support of outside stakeholders in political and judicial controversies gives them an additional advantage in the give-and-take transactions.

Managers' power to immunize themselves from outsiders is virtually unchecked and in practice it appears almost as if they have residual rights to change the rules of the game. Non-voting shares, cross-holdings (which deny

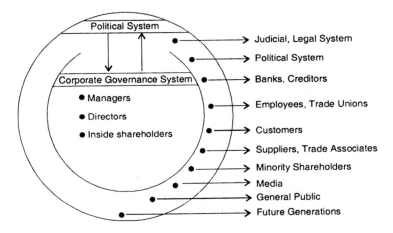

control to outside shareholders), anti-takeover measures and changes in corporate charter are some of the measures used by incumbent managers for this purpose.

Interests of various outside stakeholders get articulated with varying degrees of precision. However, minority shareholders are the most hapless group among them as they are scattered, disorganized, suffer from the problem of 'free riding' and get little sympathy from anyone. The political system too, is a stakeholder in its own right in this arrangement. It represents interests of groups such as shop-keepers, real estate agents and it is a proxy for general public. It has a financial interest in corporate governance system ranging from corporate income tax and other tax revenues to contributions to election campaign funds. The corporate governance system also provides it with a possible outlet for financing activities which would cause embarrassment if they were to appear as state budget allocations.

Political economy of corporate governance means the linkage of corporate governance with and its regulation by these political considerations or by alliances between managers, politicians, bankers, lawyers etc. which help to cement insider control and to make external investor monitoring ineffective. The main hypothesis of this model is that corporate governance systems are to be understood basically with the help of mutual exchanges among various groups. Comparative analysis of corporate governance systems treats political and judicial systems or institutions as exogenous factors. However, at least partially, they reflect the pressures of organized interests including those of corporate managements on political and judicial decision-making.

Hence mechanisms affecting the evolution of institutions must also be studied. La Porta, Shleifer et al. (1999) have inferred an inverse relationship between investor protection and ownership concentration in different countries. The relationship may actually be the result of the influence of different insiders in control in different countries and not of exogenous political and legal systems.

The proposition regarding linking together of the two systems and identification of managers' desire to insulate themselves from outsiders as the key variable behind various moves and changes finds support from different quarters. For example, in Germany, banks and managers exchange proxy votes for banks' service fees. In Germany and Switzerland, legal provisions require banks to use proxy votes in favour of corporate management unless they have explicit instructions to the contrary. In Switzerland, the Union Bank of Switzerland introduced 'name shares' in 1975 which gave management a right to refuse transfer of ownership in them without assigning any reason. These shares were abolished only in 1990 when the adverse political implications of this additional managerial discretion were realized. In Germany, legal provisions discriminate against minority shareholders. (Consider the view of a German banker, Carl Furstenberg (1850 – 1933): 'Shareholders are stupid and impertinent – stupid because they give their money to somebody else without any effective control over what this person is doing with it and impertinent because they ask for a dividend as a reward for their stupidity.') Also a shareholder or a coordinated group of shareholders can have maximum 3% to 5% of the total voting rights in Germany. The celebrated main bank system in Japan is under attack because managers wish to avoid dependence on any one bank and so they go out of their way to cultivate multiple banking relations. In the USA, regulation of corporate governance is more in favour of outside shareholders but only media exposures (which have mostly short-term impact), takeover waves and legislative changes appear to challenge the network of contacts in the corporate governance system. Even then, the political system and the judiciary reacted adversely to the takeover movement of the 1980s.

The regulation of corporate governance system by political considerations has important distributional consequences. Anyone with an eye on a firm's funds, will be opposed to distributing them to shareholders, whether in the form of dividends or takeover premium. The interest of different stakeholders is directly opposed to the interest of shareholders in getting their money back and deciding for themselves the most suitable reinvestment opportunities for them. For example, workers want managers to build up reserves and avoid or delay or at least sweeten-up possible layoffs. (This is similar to Jensen's free cash flow theory.)

There are two other consequences of political regulation of corporate governance. One, secrecy cloaks the informal give-and-take mentioned above. There is no transparency. Secrecy also serves to reduce the accountability of various parties. Second, the system becomes, more or less, a closed system which looks at outsiders with suspicion and which keeps out innovation. There are few shocks or surprises and everyone knows what punishment will be meted out for untoward behaviour. So a bias for repeating known activities is generated.

The degree of influence of different groups of insiders and outsiders varies from one system to another. So some adaptation of this model to a particular reality is necessary. At the same time, the model shows us how changes in any corporate governance system and the direction of change are to be interpreted. It is therefore a dynamic model. Also, it has a broad sweep as compared to the narrow focus of agency theory.

Both the political economy model and the principal-agent model look at managerial behaviour as the main corporate governance problem. Both agree tacitly that unseating managers is difficult and perhaps this problem has only a temporary solution. Agency theory looks at managerial opportunism while the political economy model concentrates on managerial efforts to gain greater autonomy. The difference between the two models is that the political economy model posits that managers have different principals with varying degrees of influence at their command. Thus small shareholders are principals only in name. Instead of the conflict between managers and principals, the political economy model avers that conflict between inside and outside stakeholders is the key to understanding corporate governance-system and that conflict is a big problem.

Both the principal-agent model and the political economy model have similar policy implications: limit managerial autonomy and strengthen the position of minority shareholders. Since managers are very powerful, both market and legislation (with effective enforcement) are necessary for taming managers. Both the models can be said to support market-control perspective.

Conclusion

Each of the above models, theories and approaches offers some important insight into corporate governance. At the same time, each fails in giving a complete picture. Hence an eclectic approach is essential. Out of the three approaches, capital market control approach is predominant today. A developed market is the most advanced economic mechanism known to us and it seems inevitable that other mechanisms with recede once market mechanism gets established. So organization-control perspective has probably become dated. New ideas from stakeholder-control perspective will be gradually accepted if they are introduced through the market mechanism.

5

Indian Corporate Governance: A Review

The Indian corporate governance system shows some features of the Anglo-American system and at the same time, it shares some important characteristics of the German-Japanese system. The share of small investors in corporate equity is about 40 percent — comparable with that in the USA. Inter-corporate holdings, directors', promoters' share in equity are also significant. Business groups or networks continue to control much of the private sector. The capital market has started developing only in the last two decades. These characteristics bring Indian corporate governance closer to the German – Japanese system. (See *Appendix* for a comparison of the break-up of equity holding in different countries.) The Indian system is now veering towards the Anglo-American system. To understand the Indian system, we have to trace its evolution since 1850 AD.

Historical Heritage: The Beginning

The first Indian companies came into existence around 1650 AD in South India. Plenty of trade in cotton textiles existed between India and Europe in the seventeenth century. European companies encouraged Indian merchants who used to procure supplies from weavers to form joint stock companies so that they could avoid dealing with a large number of small merchants. This idea caught on and between 1660 and 1720, many such companies were established. By 1800 however, they had all but disappeared from the scene.

Both trading and manufacturing existed in India of course, much before this time. The factory system of production was introduced around 1850 in cotton textiles and jute industries. Large scale extraction of coal, iron ore etc. also started in mines around this time. Industrial goods such as cutlery, paper, cloth and clothing, iron implements for farming, tools for house building, boats and ships etc. were produced earlier by craftsmen in small workshops. However, as far as the emergence of joint stock companies was concerned, trading came first, followed by agency business and manufacturing.

The British East India Company monopolized trade between India and other countries till 1834. Then India was opened to other British traders and trading companies. However, employees of the East India Company were not permitted to engage in private trade. So many of them resigned from the company and took up commercial and agency business. This was the beginning of agency houses which gradually came to combine trading with manufacturing, banking, bill broking and insurance.

The first managing agency in India was British. It was established in 1809. Carr, Tagore & Company (1834) is known as the first equal partnership between European and Indian businessmen and it also initiated the managing agency system in India. From then on, for over a century, growth of joint stock companies and managing agencies was simultaneous and the latter completely dominated the business economy of India.

In 1850, an Act was passed for the registration of companies with limited liability. Older businesses and business guilds did not take to the new form of organization. On the other hand, new trading and banking companies were continuously formed and they started growing. Therefore, 1850 marks a point of departure in the history of Indian business.

Agency houses found the joint stock form convenient to attract savings from a large number of investors. New companies also needed promoters who had both finance and prestige to attract other investors. Agency houses could also provide valuable services in contacting the European market. Therefore companies and managing agencies had a complementary existence. Instead of Board of Directors, managing agencies played the central governance role in these companies.

Managing agents in Europe were paid servants and they looked after only the operating side of business. In India, they had to primarily provide finance since both banking and capital markets were in a rudimentary stage of evolution. Thus managing agents usually provided a sizeable portion of initial capital. In return, they held deferred shares with disproportionate voting rights. They made all the important decisions in business on the strength of the managing agency agreement. By 1913, they controlled the majority of jute and cotton mills, tea gardens and coal mines in the country.

Because of managing agents' total grip over the companies, shareholders and directors were powerless before them. The agents enjoyed long tenures and they ensured that companies would remain in their control long after they had been set on a firm footing and the agents had reduced their own holding to insignificant proportions.

Because of managing agency system, corporate control and power did not remain with individual companies. It got vested in the parent companies – managing agents. Through inter-corporate investments and interlocking directorships, managing agents could control large business networks. Until 1914, these networks comprised mostly trading and industrial companies. Between 1915 and 1947 – a high degree of interlocking between industrial companies and banks could be seen. The macroeconomic situation around this time was marked by lax government regulation, fragmented credit system and underdeveloped capital market.

Managing agents gradually started engaging in a number of malpractices the notable among them being:

1   Investment of one company's surplus in others with the same agent and thus perpetuating many sick and at times, insolvent companies while depriving others of justifiable growth opportunities.
2   Ensuring that it was impossible to remove them, once the agency agreement was signed.
3   Subordination of company interest to agent's interest.

Managing agents were basically interested in trade and intermediation. They derived their income in the form of commission and fees. Many agents used to draw commission on purchases as well as sales effected by their companies plus an office allowance. Banks used to insist on the managing agent's guarantee before giving advance/loan to a company. So they used to earn a guarantee commission also. There were many instances of alliances between banks and managing agents, both often belonging to the same group. The result was that business was dominated by financial rather than genuinely industrial concerns.

Under these circumstances, the managed companies could not develop any kind of autonomy. Their share prices fluctuated on the basis of their managing agents' financial position. This led to plenty of speculation on Bombay (now Mumbai) and Ahmedabad Stock Exchanges. The divergence of interest between managing agents and the rest of the shareholders was very often apparent.

Managing agents denied any basic voice to other shareholders. To minimize shareholder participation, they used to establish firms themselves and then sell out their stake to new shareholders. Because of inter-corporate investments, shareholders of a profitable company could be forced to finance losses of other companies or put up risk capital for new ventures. Agents also used to acquire stakes of foreign investors who wanted to withdraw from Indian companies. These stakes were often acquired at high premia, were financed from the coffers of the company controlled by agents and details of these deals were seldom provided to shareholders. In addition, managing agents also took the following steps to limit shareholder participation:

a   controlling the issue of securities so as to limit public participation in company affairs,
b   inserting special conditions so that for example, debentures issued by one company were subscribed to mainly by other companies in the network.

Among the British businessmen in India, there were simply not enough persons by the end of the nineteenth century to constitute Boards of Directors of all the companies floated by them. So multiple directorships became the practice. Consequently, Indian companies did not have on their boards the experience and variety of interests needed for successful and efficient direction. The few Indians nominated to the boards under British managing agents became 'stock' directors of all companies. In 1950–51, 9 leading Indian industrial families held 600 directorships, with only Dalmia and Singhania holding 200 of them. One hundred individuals were found to hold 1700 directorships, 30 of them holding 860 directorships and the top 10–400 directorships.

This type of multiple directorships led to weakening of responsibility. The role of director used to be any way extremely limited. The rubber stamp nature of Indian boards has continued in the post-independence period.

The managing agency system dominated the Indian business world upto independence. It was formally abolished in 1969. Indian business families took over the essence of the system and combined it with non-transparent, intra-family property holding. Till date, in each business group, an investment company (companies) acts as the agency through which control is exercised over all the firms belonging to the group.

Managing agents' practice of owning a small portion of equity and splitting the rest into small lots to garner all proxy votes necessary for control has created a continuing tradition of control with insignificant ownership. Thus until recently, all prominent business families have controlled 'their' companies on the basis of minor ownership holdings. As pointed out by RK Hazari in 1966, there were some differences among them in this respect. For example, Tata and Martin Burn had smaller controlling blocks while companies in Birla, Dalmia, Bangur, Thapar, JK and Mafatlal groups were more closely held and controlled. In the liberalized era that began in 1992, promoters have felt threatened and all have increased and consolidated their holdings.

Historical Heritage: Independence to 1980s

After 1951, an ambitious programme of planned industrial development with the public sector at the commanding heights of the economy and with extensive government controls began. In 1964, the government appointed Monopolies Inquiry Commission (MIC) to look into the phenomenon of concentration of economic power in industry. MIC defined product-wise, industry-wise and country-wise concentration and it found that in a majority of products analyzed by it, concentration was high. It also collected data on industrial groups. This was not easy as nominee (*benami*) shareholding was widespread and identity of true shareholders was covered up. It concluded that 75 out of the 83 business groups for which it collected data accounted for 44 per cent of the total paid up capital of the private sector. It also noted instances of pre-emptive action (e.g. preventing competitors from entering particular fields) by industrialists. MIC's overall conclusion was that concentration of economic power had increased since 1950. It held the managing agency system, actual operation of industrial licensing system and government control over capital issues, foreign exchange and imports responsible for this outcome. (Government control was ostensibly for reducing the power of business groups but its outcome was the opposite.)

Professor RK Hazari analyzed the ownership and control patterns of some 1000 companies in the private sector between 1951 and 1958. He noted the following:

- Public limited companies relied more on debt rather than equity, on fixed rather than working capital. So their net worth barely covered their fixed assets.
- Tata, Martin Burn and the Shri Ram groups concentrated most of their assets in a few large companies whereas Birla, Dalmia, Sahu Jain, Bangur and JK groups dispersed them over a large number of companies.
- Dispersion of ownership and/or reluctance of large investors (as in Kirloskar, Seshasayee, Mahindra groups) to participate in management, enabled controlling interests to retain control. In case of Tata Iron and Steel Co. Ltd., large holding of LIC and implicit support of government helped Tata group to retain control in spite of low shareholding.

Professor Hazari's concluded that through the mechanisms of holding companies and interlocking directorships, business families had built, intermeshed and pyramidal structures of control which they continued to consolidate. In fact, industrial concentration had increased during this period. Professor Hazari also made an analysis of licensing applications. It showed clearly that business groups, particularly the Birla group, used them to foreclose licensable capacity in key products to competitors.

Dutt Committee or the Industrial Licensing Policy Inquiry Committee (1969) made a major contribution in this respect. Hazari – Dutt thesis was that Indian oligopoly was stable due to its financial strength, market power and most important, its ability to use state intervention for erecting an external barrier to entry. To counter the concentration of economic power in the oligopoly, Dutt Committee recommended a policy of confining larger groups and foreign companies to core and heavy industries. It also recommended that public sector financial institutions should be used to bring about a structural change in ownership and control of the private sector. So public financial institutions were asked to participate in the management and control of assisted firms. Appointment of nominee directors and option to convert all or part of their advances into equity were to be the instruments for achieving this objective.

Because of popular pressure exerted by these reports, the Monopolies and Restrictive Trade Practices (MRTP) Act was passed in 1970 and the MRTP Commission was set up. In June 1977 it became mandatory for public financial institutions to put the convertibility clause and nominee directors' appointment clause in their loan agreements. Nominee directors were to be appointed on the boards of companies which had availed of substantial assistance which was defined as advance exceeding Rs. 50 lakh in 1971 and after periodic revision, the figure came to Rs.500 lakh in 1984. In case of these large borrowings, public financial institutions had the option to convert 20% of the excess into equity of the borrowing company.

After nationalisation of 14 major commercial banks in the country, development finance became the prime objective of banking sector. Business promoters were precluded from owning more than 40 per cent of equity in their businesses. The same limit applied to foreign companies also and in 1973 they had to make public equity offers for diluting their holdings.

Therefore by the early 1980s, public financial institutions came to supply long term debt to corporate sector and held a insignificant share of its equity. However, the scenario foreseen by The Dutt Committee remained illusive in real terms. A lot of political pressure was put on public financial institutions and they were given to understand that they were to support existing promoters as far as possible. Courts tended to favour alleged preferential rights of existing promoters irrespective of their track record. Therefore these institutions could not attempt to monitor corporate performance.

It has been remarked earlier that business networks and absence of a strong capital market ensured that Indian corporate governance system turned out to be different from Anglo-American system. Large-scale state intervention since 1951, as detailed above, made the departure even more marked. Financial assistance by public financial institutions has been mentioned above. In addition, there was direct government control over issue of securities, appointment of directors, their remuneration etc. The extent of state subsidization was also substantial. For example, most of the advances by public financial institutions were at concessional rates of interest.

These features pulled India corporate governance more towards German corporate governance and Japapese or East Asian corporate governance system. These systems have all along been characterized by large-scale state subsidization of industry. However, there was one crucial difference. In east Asian economies, there existed a strict quid pro quo between state and private capital: every assistance by the state was matched by compliance with performance standards by private capital. In India, on the other hand, state helped the accumulation of surplus without specifying or requiring any performance standards by capital. The unidirectional relationship between state and capital was strengthened progressively and it became more open and blatant over the years. Development banking in India is the best example of this absence of reciprocity.

Till 1992, public financial institutions and banks followed the practice of taking credit in their profit and loss, account for interest not actually received. The presumption was that eventually all dues would be recovered because of underlying government guarantee. The extent of bad debts, poorly performing or non-performing assets was not openly reckoned. Public financial institutions had no incentive for undertaking important work, such as, regular examination of portfolios and finding poorly performing accounts. Non-performing assets started going up also because of political pressure and corrupt practices of bank officials. Roy made a study of 99 firms from cotton textiles, engineering, chemicals and other industries from 1979–83 and concluded that the performance of firms where financial institutions were large and 'real' equity holders was worse than others and that with a rise in institutional holding, concerned firms became more inefficient. This was because there was easy availability of funds but no serious monitoring by financial institutions.

Thus over-leveraged firms belonging to one business group or another – this was the representative picture of Indian companies in the 1980s. There was cheap state finance and a protected home market for goods. This combination brought about "an inefficient and flabby industrial structure of agglomerative firms under family control, with fragmented capacities and without economies of scale, largely stagnant technologically, dependent on the state for finance and protected market, hemmed in by the straitjacket of controls in literally every aspect of the economy, with little experience of real competition and with a vested interest in an economy of scarcity and shortage which the system of controls had provided." (Nayar, 1998) Industrialists and promoters very much wanted internal liberalization (i.e. freedom from state control) but not external liberalization. Public financial institutions continued to advance money and industrial sickness became rampant. Sickness then spread to the financial sector also.

A report in *The Economic Times* (11-9-1988) analyzed the causes of industrial sickness as follows:

Cause	% to total
1 Mismanagement including diversion of funds, infighting and lack of marketing strategy	52
2 Market recession	23
3 Faulty planning and technical drawbacks	14
4 Labour trouble	2
5 Others e.g. shortage of raw material, power cuts etc.	9
Total	100

LC Gupta (1988) has made the following typology of causes of sickness:
- operating sickness
- strategic sickness caused by lack of adaptability to long-term environmental change
- staying power deficiency caused by detective financial structure
- still-born i.e. wrongly conceived cases
- catastrophic sickness.

He has stated that nearly half of the sick businesses in India were operationally sick and further half of them were sick due to managerial corruption. Thus a quarter of the sick businesses had reached that state due to corruption, pure and simple. Inter-corporate investments were the main mechanism through which a corrupt management diverted corporate funds into personal/family coffers. Other common malpractices adopted by corrupt management are:

- channel to sales, purchases, transport and construction contracts, repairs, advertising etc. through family owned firms
- accepting short weight or inferior quality from suppliers in return for kick-backs
- over-invoicing of imports and under- invoicing of exports
- selling good production as seconds
- extravagant perquisites.

In case of sick companies, neither of the following options was pursued.

a takeover – merger – reorganization
b liquidation – exit

Instead companies chose the Board for Industrial and Financial Reconstruction (BIFR) route. BIFR was created for making utmost efforts to keep sick units alive at public expense. It has been aptly remarked that in spite of a staggering number of sick companies in the economy, there are no sick promoters or business groups.

The few hostile takeovers that were seen in this period were thwarted by promoters on the basis of their equity holding up to 40 percent. Reputed promoters with smaller equity holding cleverly used notions of goodwill, patriotism, Swadeshi etc. and managed to retain control. The most striking feature of the corporate scene in the late 1980s was that business promoters continued to control their firms fearing neither any monitoring from public financial institutions nor any disciplining through take-ever bids in the capital market.

The capital market started growing rapidly in the 1980s, mainly as a source of finance for large corporations. Debenture issues were very popular then for raising capital. According to Hanson (1999), the capital market served as an escape valve from the repressed banking system for large corporations during this period. However, there were a number of problems such as – limited information and transparency, individual dealer-based trading system making the ascertainment of actual price at which securities were traded difficult and lower price of initial public offerings.

So the capital market scarcely performed its normal function of providing accurate security prices to enable investors to judge the profitability of various firms.

From 1990 Till Date

In the package of economic reforms initiated in 1991, financial sector reforms were in the forefront. Narasimha Committee submitted its report in November 1991 and shortly afterwards, the government indicated a broad acceptance of its approach.

Then a process of rapid reforms in the capital market and banking sector was set in motion.

The main thrust of the financial liberalization package was to remove direct government control of the financial system. Instead, a new regime of greater disclosure, transparency and indirect control was to be ushered in under an independent market regulator. Accordingly, Securities Exchange Board of India (SEBI), originally established in 1988, was elevated in 1992 to the level of capital market regulator. Capital Issues Control Act, 1947 was scrapped. So companies could have free access to capital market and they could price their security issues freely, subject only to SEBI conditions. In 1993, capital market was opened to foreign institutional investors. Simultaneously, Indian companies were allowed to raise capital abroad by issuing Global Depository Receipts (GDRs) and other instruments. The National Stock Exchange (NSE) was set up in 1994 as an automated electronic exchange. Because of it, a single, nationwide market in securities covering 150 cities has emerged. Over the Counter Exchange of India (OTCEI) became operational for serving the interests of smaller companies. National Securities Depository Ltd. (NSDL) was opened in 1996. It provides for electronic transfer of ownership of securities from one account to another. Buy-back of shares was permitted in 1999 on the basis of an amendment to companies Act.

Various changes in the financial system are summarized in the following table:

Table 5.1. *Changes in financial system*

Changes in corporate governance system	Macroeconomic changes
Free pricing of shares	Deregulation of capital market
Buyback of shares	Deregulation of banking sector
Foreign ownership of equity	Deregulation of trade policy
Reduction of capital control	Convertibility of the current and
Relaxation on limits to	capital account
expansion and diversification	Repeal of the Foreign Exchange
of corporate bodies.	Regulation Act (FERA)
	Liberalization of foreign
	Investments

(SEBI had to impose many restrictions on equity issue pricing. So control over capital issues could not be done away with.)
(Source: A Mukherjee Reed, 2001)

As soon as control on capital issues was lifted and free pricing of shares was allowed, a stock market boom started. People rushed to buy shares and many companies came up with new issues. Preferential allotments were used by business promoters, in the atmosphere of heightened expectations that followed, to increase their holdings at prices substantially lower than market prices. In many cases preferential shares were allotted only to help promoters to increase their stake in the companies and there were no long-term plans for investing the amount raised.

The number of new issues in the primary market was 455 in 1991–92 and the amount of capital raised was Rs. 9441 crore. In 1994–95, there were 1686 new issues which mopped up Rs. 37,328 crore or a four-times higher amount. Then investors' sentiments were reversed due to a number of frauds and scams and there was a sharp drop in the amount raised. In 1997–98, there were only 156 new issues totaling Rs. 11,859 crore. As it became difficult to raise finance, private placements became popular. They involve a private sale of debt or equity by a company, rather than a public offering through the capital market. The amount raised through private placement increased from Rs. 424 crore in 1990–91 to Rs. 4966 crore in 1998–99. The largest private placement deal in the country involved Reliance Industries Ltd. and three major public institutions viz. UTI, LIC and GIC in 1994. By virtue of this transaction, Reliance Industries placed its shares with these institutions at a price much higher than the market price with a 5 year lock-in period. This amounted to a grave misuse of public funds.

Dubious practices of Indian businesses reached a peak around mid-1990s in the atmosphere of freedom from government controls. Preferential issues, price rigging, exorbitant pricing of new issues, accounting jugglery, lax project implementation, overpriced foreign issues – all were seen in the market. Companies such as Usha Rectifier, Bindal Agro, MS Shoes, CRB Capital Markets, Prudential Capital Markets, real value appliances, plantation companies, many companies of Modi, Singhania, Thapar and other groups made scandals and fleeced investors. Harshad Mehta became the biggest price manipulator on stock exchanges in 1992. He artificially built up the stocks of companies such as BPL, Sterlite and Videocon. In the end, names of these companies were tarnished, retail investors lost a lot of money and Mehta was put behind bars. (In 1999, Ketan Parikh took over from where Harshad Mehta had left of.)

In corporate governance literature, there exists an extreme case called *insiders' dilemma*. This is a situation where entrenchment of insiders pushes up agency costs to such an extent that outside owners and creditors refuse to supply funds to firms. Under these circumstances, the capital market cannot carry out its resource allocation task. Between 1995 and 1997, this was actually the situation in India. Till date, retail investors prefer to stay away from the stock market.

Ordinarily this would not matter in the sense, retail investors are any way expected to make available their savings through mutual funds and other intermediaries. Unfortunately, the oldest public sector mutual found in the country – Unit Trust of India (UTI), established to provide stable, reliable income to small investors became sick in 1998 and admitted that its net asset value was below Rs. 10 after 34 years of investing. Again in July 2001, UTI was caught in a crisis when it suspended the repurchase of its flagship scheme – US-64. This was the result of reckless, dubious involvement in equity issues after 1994. Other funds such as Canbank Mutual Fund (linked with Harshad Mehta), BOI Mutual Fund, Indbank Mutual Fund followed in the footsteps of UTI.

Thus liberalization and deregulation of capital market gave an impetus to bad loans by banks and mindless equity investments by mutual funds. These resulted in unprecedented scams. In retrospect, the abolition of capital issues control looks like a hasty move. In the subsequent upheaval, small investors lost money as well as hope and confidence. Private promoters however, made windfall profits. Provisions such as buyback of shares, raising the quota of promoters' contribution in total capital, making inter corporate investments without government permission helped them further. In contrast, no attempt was made to strengthen the monitoring mechanism in the Companies Act. SEBI is gradually taking corrective measures but these are usually put in place after much harm has taken place.

Investors who rushed to the capital market for the first time in the 1990s have found that an estimated 30 to 40 per cent of the companies floated in the boom years of 1991 to 1994 no longer exist. In fact '*vanishing companies*' is a regular phenomenon and it is an outright fraud on shareholders.

The number of companies in India has multiplied since 1992. The number is currently above 4.5 lakh, double the number in 1990–91. Out of these 4.5 lakh companies, barely 10,000 are listed companies and 2 lakh companies do not file annual tax returns. Most of the companies fall in the category of non-listed, private limited companies. In the last decade, the number of trading, investment and construction companies has increased while the number of manufacturing companies has declined. There exist network of promoters behind many companies. Indian promoters are adept at floating new companies for effecting transfers, for making adjustments to reduce their tax liability and for consolidating their control. The multiplication of companies since 1991 therefore does not represent a genuine upsurge of entrepreneurship except in information technology sector.

Stock exchanges in India suffer from some basic problems. The incidence of actual deliveries of shares is low in keeping with the speculative nature of dealing on them. Secondly, transactions and price index are both dominated by group A companies. Ninety three per cent of value traded and 76.3 per cent of transactions on BSE in 1999 comprised top 100 companies. At the same time, there are many companies whose securities are not traded at ail. These and below-par trading companies (See Table 5.2) which account for nearly two-third of all listed companies show the extent of sickness in the corporate sector and also the quality of new public issues.

The secondary capital market was dormant till the 1990s. There were very few takeovers and mergers. In the large, protected home market, oligopolies did not compete with each other openly. Diversification was the preferred strategy. So

Table 5.2. *Incidence of below par trading at BSE*

Last traded price per share	1997		1998	
	No. of companies	% of total	No. of companies	% of total
Not traded	831	14.22	1805	30.84
Below Rs. 5	2853	48.83	2041	34.88
Rs. 5 to Rs. 10	673	11.52	644	11.00
Sub Total	**4357**	**74.57**	**4490**	**76.73**
Rs. 10 and above	1486	25.43	1362	23.27
Total	**5843**	**100.00**	**5852**	**100.00**

(Source: Rao, Murthy, Ranganathan, 1999)

hostile takeovers were not necessary, nor would they have fitted into the logic of power sharing between politicians, bureaucrats and industrialists. The Indian Companies Act, 1956 allowed corporate boards the right to refuse transfer of shares to particular buyers provided the proposed transfer went either against company or public interest. Therefore hostile takeovers were not possible also.

Now this situation has changed. Each year the number of mergers and takeovers is increasing. There were just 30 to 35 mergers in the late 1980s. Then the number went up to 430 in 1995 and 552 in 1997. Entry of foreign portfolio investment, presence of a large number of sick companies and removal of curbs on concentration are the reasons behind this increase. SEBI has prepared a takeover code under SEBI (Substantial Acquisition of Shares and Takeovers) Regulations in 1994. The code has been modified subsequently to make changes easier. As per the code, banks and financial institutions are not allowed to finance takeovers. Leveraged buy-outs (LBOs) or takeover defenses such as poison pills are not permitted. The code permits block holders to make creeping acquisition and the most important provision of the code is that in case of changes in control which affect more than 15 per cent of total stake in a company, a mandatory public offer has to be made.

Changes in Company Finance

Along with the changes traced above and particularly with the transformation of the financial system from bank to capital market domination, different sources in the finances of Indian firms has changed. The share of reserves and surplus in project finance has declined continuously and is now negligible. Indian firms rely almost exclusively on external finance. (External finance refers to funds raised externally and includes both borrowed funds and share capital.) See Table. 5.3 in the following page.

Table 5.3. *Financing of project cost of companies*

Source	% share of sources		
	1971–72 to 1980–81	1981–82 to 1990–91	1991–92 to 1995–96
Number of companies	83	319	530
a Share capital – Indian	28.5	37.5	41.1
of which equity capital	26.5	37.5	41.0
b Share capital – Foreign	0.2	0.1	5.5
c Reserves and surplus	11.8	3.4	1.6
d Loans, of which:	53.3	39.6	45.3
Financial institutions	24.1	22.5	12.1
Banks	15.5	6.6	10.0
Promoters, directors, friends	0.6	1.0	8.7
e Debentures, bonds	4.5	18.2	6.1
f Miscellaneous	1.7	1.2	0.4
Total	**100.00**	**100.00**	**100.00**

(Source: Joseph, Nitsure and Subnavis, 1999)

What leaps to the eye is the continuous increase in equity capital in these 25 years. Finance from debenture and bond issues increased in the 1980s but went down subsequently. Companies have reduced their borrowings and among borrowings, dependence on financial institutions has gone down but that on promoters has gone up. Another study however, shows that among external funds, borrowings have been preferred by Indian companies.

Businesses in developed countries are found to rely primarily on internal sources of finance. One study (quoted by Joseph, Nitsure et al.) showed that during 1970–85, internal funds made up almost two-third of investment financing in the USA, the UK, Japan, Germany, France, Italy, Canada and Finland. External funding accounted for less than 10 per cent of total investment expenditure in these countries. In the UK and the USA, businesses use more equity while Germany and Japan rely more on bank finance. This is in keeping with greater importance given to capital market and banks respectively in these countries in the process of development.

Greater use of internal finance enhances managerial discretion. Lenders generally demand higher interest as they have less information, as compared to managers, available with them to judge credit risk. So internal funds are cheaper, too. Internal finance gives a measure of autonomy to business growth and so in the developed countries, a clear pecking order is seen in firms for raising finance: internal finance as far as possible, then debt and equity is the last resort. In these countries, it is observed that the price of outstanding shares drops whenever a firm announces new equity issue. Debt issue too, has a similar but weak effect.

There is a sharp difference between developed and developing countries on this score. Firms in developing countries use less internal finance. In external finance, macroeconomic factors decide whether they will lean on the side of borrowings or equity. It was found, in a comparative study of American and Indian firms' finances, that the proportion of external equity was comparable in both and the difference boiled down to a lower use of internal finance and higher use of borrowings in Indian firms. The study is based on data from 1972–92 and since the Indian financial system was a bank-based one during this period, the finding is intuitively plausible. D'Souza explains the reliance of Indian firms on borrowings in the following manner:

Induction of more debt in the capital structure of a firm gives rise to two opposite effects – one value-enhancing, the other – value-reducing. With the availability of more funds, a firm can produce more and edge out its competitors in an oligopolistic product market. This adds value. At the same time, with more borrowed funds, residual returns to shareholders become uncertain and a conflict may arise between lenders and shareholders. It reduces firm value. D'Souza observes that value-reducing effect is weak in India and so additional borrowings have enhanced firm value. Till 1991, the state gave an implicit assurance to maintain stability and viability of the banking sector. If a firm failed to honour its commitments, banks bore the cost (and accumulated huge non-performing assets!). Firms took a continuous flow of bank credit for granted and followed expansionary policies which resulted in their dominant positions in the protected product markets.

After 1992, this has changed. Government protection of financial system is considerably reduced and banks have started using screening and risk-assessment techniques seriously to bring down their NPAs.

The primary issues market has gradually become important in India after 1980. First large companies tapped it for debenture issues. Then the cult of equity spread quickly and all types of firms flocked to the market. In other developing countries also, reliance on equity was induced by government policy. Unlike in India, stock markets in these countries have been developed by the government. Singh and Hamid however, point out that capital market development in developing countries has not given rise to a net increase in gross domestic savings or to the proportion of financial savings and so has not yet made a real contribution to development.

Indian Corporate Governance System Today

The Indian Companies Act, 1956 with continuing amendments, SEBI, secondary capital market or market for corporate control and financial institutions and institutional investors are the main parts of the corporate governance system. The Indian Companies Act, fashioned on the lines of the British company law, has provided the formal structure of corporate governance. Its primary objective is to give adequate protection to shareholders and creditors. The extent of government control on various aspects of corporate existence has been progressively reduced. The Act grants the following rights to shareholders to enforce managerial accountability:

- Every shareholder has the right to vote on every resolution placed in shareholders' annual meeting— and to vote for deciding the composition of board of directors.
- Proxy voting and postal ballot are permitted.
- All shares carry proportional voting rights.
- Every company has to annually hold a general body meeting called Annual General Meeting (AGM). The Board of Directors can convene an extraordinary general meeting.
- Board of directors is a one-tier body comprising a chairman, and/or managing director, executive and non-executive directors. There exists a special category of wholetime directors. Every public limited company must have minimum 3 directors.
- Shareholders must receive audited financial statements of their company. They also have a right to retain their proportional ownership in the company.
- Rights of minority shareholders are on par with those in other countries.

The Companies (Amendment) Act, 2000 has provided that, apart from postal ballot for specified matters, small shareholders will have their director on board of directors. It has sought to protect small investors. For small companies, it has prescribed secretarial audit and has mandated audit committees of board of directors for large companies. It has permitted issue of equity shares with differential rights as to dividend and voting. It has pegged the maximum number of directorships at 15.

SEBI has gradually evolved a regulatory framework, with rules governing functioning of stock exchanges, brokers, merchant bankers etc. It has tried to modify the governing structure of stock exchanges to make their boards more broad-based and to reduce the dominance of brokers in their working.

SEBI's takeover code has already been mentioned. It has made the following additions to listing agreement (agreement between stock exchanges and companies desirous of listing their securities on them):

- stronger disclosure norms for initial public offers
- declaration of unaudited quarterly results
- mandatory appointment of **compliance officer** to monitor share transfer process
- director's report to give information about variation between projected and actual use of funds etc.

As per the recommendations of the Kumar Mangalam Birla Committee appointed by it (2000), SEBI has added Clause 49 to listing agreement. This clause stipulates that listed companies have to comply with conditions regarding the right mix of executive and non executive directors in composing Board of Directors, formation of audit committee and investors' grievance committee, holding board meetings, inclusion of Management Discussion and Analysis section in the annual report, auditor's certification in the annual report regarding compliance with various corporate governance provisions etc. These conditions have become binding on all companies since March 2003.

The market for corporate control has slowly started picking up momentum now. There are plenty of regulations and restrictions on its working. The day when, through aggressive, hostile takeovers it will start working as monitoring mechanism of the last resort is far away. Some analysts of the Indian situation have stated that codes of desirable practices rules and regulations are inadequate and ineffective here and what is needed is governance by force and market forces. We are moving in that direction but even in the USA, the kind of surge in takeover activity that was seen in the mid-1980s is over since long and SEC's regulations do the monitoring job.

Financial institutions and institutional investors will continue to be partners in corporate governance arrangement but they will have to function in a responsible, discreet and selective manner. Even nominee directors of public financial institutions should continue to contribute for improving the quality of corporate governance. The kind of contribution that foreign institutional investors can make was seen in Wipro's ADR issue in 2000. At their and SEC's insistence; A Premji's stake of over 75% of equity had to be highlighted as a **risk factor.** Otherwise in India, it would have never been mentioned or worse, it would have been touted as a plus factor and gullible investors would have ended up paying a premium for their disempowerment!

To conclude, the Indian corporate governance system is in a transition, towards the Anglo-American corporate governance with a strong capital market. Market control perspective is as yet quite distinct to this system and its hybrid nature because of features from other corporate governance system will also remain there for some more time. Given the historical evolution of the system and its complexity, such an outcome is unavoidable.

Appendix

Some Data on Equity Ownership

Table 5.4. *Break-up of equity ownership in different countries*

Distribution of Shareholding	India (1996)	USA	UK	Germany (1993)	Japan
Financial corporations	9.8	46	62	29	4
Non-Financial corporations	23.8	–	2	39	2
a all corporations	33.6	46	64	68	6
b Individuals	40.9	49	18	17	2
c Foreign	10.1	5	16	12	–
d Government	–	–	1	4	–
e others (directors, promoters)	15.4	–	2	–	–
Total	**100.00**	**100**	**100**	**100**	**100**

(Source: Sarkar and Sarkar, 1999.)

Table 5.5. *Equity ownership in different types of companies in India in 1995–96*

Equity holding by	Private Companies		Foreign Companies		All
	Belonging to business groups	Stand alone companies	Belonging to business groups	Stand alone companies	
Public	34.5	46.4	22.4	30.0	40.9
Corporate bodies	33.5	18.5	18.3	14.0	23.8
Directors and relatives	8.2	21.3	0.8	2.8	15.4
Foreign investors	9.3	7.4	42.0	43.1	10.1
Institutional investors (LIC, GIC, UTI)	10.3	3.2	12.2	8.4	6.2
Financial institutions (IDBI, ICICI, IFCI)	4.2	3.2	4.3	1.7	3.6
Total	100.0	100.0	100.0	100.0	100.0

(Source: Sarkar and Sarkar, 1999, based on a sample of 1567 manufacturing companies in the private sector.)

Part II

6

Board of Directors: The Topmost Internal Governance Mechanism

Introduction

A bulk of current corporate governance literature revolves around the Board of Directors and its functioning. Two recurring themes on Board of Directors are – weak boards being responsible for corporate excesses and failures in the 1980s and 1990s, there is a wide divergence between the theory about board's work and its actual functioning.

As regards the first theme, lack of balance due to paucity of appropriate skills, lack of commitment, inadequate information, inadequate systems of financial control, over-dominance of CEOs, their short-term policies designed to increase profits rather than real earnings etc. have been identified as important problems in the working of boards. In theory, shareholders of a company elect the board which nominates managers to carry on work. In reality, top managers often select a team of directors which is approved by shareholders and which often works at the pleasure of managers. (This was truer of the USA than of the UK or India.) Therefore, it came to be strongly believed that the highest internal mechanism of corporate monitoring was not working as it should, principally because there was little distance between managers and directors. So all the working groups and committees on corporate governance have devoted maximum attention to the working of boards and to making suggestions for improvements in them. Every aspect of the board– its election, composition, size, working style and functioning, access to information, effectiveness etc. – has been scrutinized to find out ways for improvement.

In the USA, boards were under the control of powerful CEOs till the 1980s. Now many directors are willing to play a rather proactive role. This follows the exhortations of different committees and examples set by boards of companies such as General Motors, Sears, Roebuck and Company, Compaq Computers etc. April 6, 1992 marks a watershed in this respect for on this date, non-executive directors of General Motors fired the CEO and restructured the senior management of the company. This move started an era of board activism in the corporate world.

Takeovers and monitoring by institutional investors are commonly treated as rival governance mechanisms. According to Williamson (1985) however, takeovers and Board of Directors substitute each other as corporate governance devices. His substitute hypothesis states that importance of the board in governance is greater in businesses which operate in markets where takeovers are difficult. In other words, a weak market for corporate control leads to a greater role by the internal monitoring mechanism viz. Board of Directors and then the board tends to be dominated by outsiders. Conversely, an active takeover market reduces the necessity for internal monitoring and then boards have a high incidence of insiders. Thus takeovers monitor board performance.

Many empirical studies support the substitute hypothesis above. Kini et al. studied 244 successful takeovers between 1958 and 1984 in the USA and classified them as disciplinary (141) and non-disciplinary (103) takeovers. They found that disciplinary takeovers led to the departure of the concerned CEOs and a significant reduction in board size as compared to non-disciplinary takeovers. They also found that disciplinary takeovers led to a high rate of departure of directors belonging to the dominant group and this brought about greater balance between inside and outside directors.

Board of Directors occupies the middle ground between shareholders and managers. It ought to have an identity distinct from both these groups. According to Fama and Jensen (1983), it is an important institution for resolving the agency problem between shareholders and managers. Mace (1971), on the other hand, is of the view that boards show little dissent from management and carry out little monitoring. A middle position is taken by Warther (1994) who argues that the board combines passive dissent with strong monitoring. Board members want to increase firm value but they also have to retain their seats on the board. So they are partially, not fully, aligned with shareholders. With the threat to sack under-performing management, a board can goad it to work better. At the same time, an unsuccessful attempt to fire management would mean that a director has to lose his own seat. So directors do not act trivially while removing managers and take their monitoring role seriously.

The relationship among managers, directors and shareholders is better understood with the help of the diagram in the following page.

The triangle is the core of corporate governance, defined in a narrow sense. Most of corporate governance reforms have concentrated on the relationship between shareholders and management on the one hand and between the board and management on the other. Between shareholders and management, more frequent reporting and greater transparency have been emphasized while efforts have been made to create greater distance between the board and management to avoid conflicts of interest. So importance has been given to formation of board

CEO and management

periodic updates, strategic directions

transparent financial reporting

company & CEO oversight

capital

weak controls, little influence

shareholders ◄──────────── Board

minimum information, no
individual accountability
(Montgomery, Kaufman, 2003)

committees and to greater contribution by independent directors. However, the relationship between shareholders and the board remains a neglected area. So an important link in governance is missing. Shareholders are mostly not in a position to give direction to the board or hold it accountable for its behaviour. Since shareholders do not matter in running the board, two tendencies are seen. Firstly, internal board dynamics take on primary importance. Secondly, directors and managers come together which results in a skewed corporate governance triangle.

The upshot is that if there is no crisis, an independent director finds it very difficult to make a contribution. Under the combined weight of CEO's preferences, majority view and expert opinion, directors learn to remain silent and not raise objections. A consensus-driven environment is produced in the boardrooms and this is one major point of criticism of present board practice. To give greater importance to the relationship between shareholders and directors, it is recommended that directors should be made individually accountable to shareholders and that shareholders should be involved in selecting new directors. So nomination committees should have greater importance and CEOs should be kept away from them. It is also suggested that separate funding should be made available to the boards for carrying out their work without remaining at the mercy of the management.

Which is the prime constituency to which Board of Directors is responsible? Is it the company or the shareholders or the stakeholders? Interestingly, different corporate governance systems and countries have given different answers to this question and the earlier Table 6.1 throws more light on this with a few more important differences. It appears that directors are primarily responsible to shareholders and occasionally to the corporate body and other stakeholders.

Usually business promoters, other block holders or majority shareholders and major creditors appoint their representatives to the Board of Directors. These directors ensure that interests of their principals are not harmed while a firm

Table 6.1. *Differences in functioning of the Board of Directors*

Feature	USA	UK	Germany	Japan
Goals and duties	To promote financial interests of shareholders	To promote financial interests of shareholders	To ensure long-term health of the company, taking stakeholders' demands into account	To ensure long-term health of the company
Structure	Unitary	Unitary	Two-tier. Only supervisory board can be compared with boards in other countries.	
Composition	80% outsiders. CEOs of other companies, academicians, lawyers etc.	40% outsiders (Non-Executive Directors) – CEOs of other companies, professionals of high rank. Dominated by insider/ executive directors.	Supervisory boards: 50% directors* elected by employees, 50% elected by shareholders. (*50% of these are trade union representatives)	Mainly insider/executive directors. Constitute the incumbent senior management. Non-Executive Directors are also there.
Size	13	12	12–22	20–30
Board leadership	Board chairman is the leader of the company.	Vested in non-executive board chairman.	Management board chairman and supervisory board chairman are different. Latter is elected by shareholders.	Usually retired company president or retired government officer. Exerts little influence on decision -making. Ceremonial
Board committees	Common and popular	Uncommon till Cadbury Committee report	Uncommon	Uncommon

(Adapted from Lorsch and Graff, 1996)

goes about operating in the market. Small or majority shareholders usually get a short shrift in the process of representation but in principle, directors are supposed to represent *all* shareholders.

To reduce agency costs, shareholders have to ensure that the board monitors the management. An early model of a board functioning (Tricker, 1984) is as follows:

	Focus on business needs	**Focus on stakeholders' needs**
Emphasis on external issues	Direction	Accountability
Emphasis on internal issues	Executive management	Supervision

Direction, accountability and supervision are the functions of board of directors. It has to oversee executive action without getting involved with operational issues. This is something all boards understand: directors universally prefer a policy of less rather than more interference with operations. Only impending or actual crises have forced their hands in this respect.

Differentiation between direction and management is built into the structure of German boards. In them, management board takes care of executive management while supervisory board looks after accountability issues and direction. Board of Directors in the USA and the UK do not follow this rigid distinction but the recent importance of non-executive directors in them is precisely for ensuring that boards do not get tied down to executive matters. Audit and other board committees, comprising mainly or exclusively non-executive directors, perform the duty of monitoring management and enforcing its accountability.

Functions of the Board

1 Reviewing and guiding corporate strategy, major plans, risk policy, business plans and annual budgets.
2 Monitoring corporate performance.
3 Overseeing major capital expenditure, acquisitions and divestitures.
4 Selection of key executives, succession planning.
5 Monitoring and managing potential conflicts of interests of management, directors and shareholders and looking out for misuse of corporate assets.
6 Monitoring the effectiveness of governance practices under which it operates and making changes as necessary.
7 Overseeing the process of disclosure and communication.

The above are specified by the OECD principles of corporate governance (1999). The following items can be added to the list:

a   declaring dividend
b   ensuring that financial information furnished to shareholders fairly presents the actual state of a affairs
c   participating actively in decisions to elect or re-elect directors.

Bain, Band (1996) quote with approval an example of Board of Director's work from the records of an FTSE 50 company. The work list neatly delineates stock exchange requirements, Companies Act requirements, the Cadbury Committee recommendations, matters dealing with management oversight, board composition and miscellaneous matter. The last category is instructive. It includes the following:

1   changes in the rules or trustees of company pension scheme
2   changes in the rules of employee option plan
3   political donations
4   prosecution, defense or settlement of litigation
5   internal control arrangements
6   environmental policy
7   directors' interest in shares, share options and external interests.

Bain and Band also point out that another FTSE 100 company had opted for a very brief statement of matters reserved for the board and it was actually making much more progress on the corporate governance front. Genuine commitment to corporate governance reforms is important rather than impressive looking documents.

The work of the board is of course, complex and the board faces many contradictory demands while doing it. Some of these demands are:

- the board must be focused on commercial needs of business and must also act responsibly towards employees, business partners and society as a whole
- it must be sensitive to the pressures of short-term issues and yet be informed about broader, long-term trends
- it must be entrepreneurial and drive the business forward while keeping it under prudent control
- it must be sufficiently knowledgeable about the working of a company and it should also be able to stand back from day-to-day management to retain an objective, detached view

Anyone with a little experience of the real world will know how difficult it is to do justice to these demands.

Role and Working

Company law maintains that shareholders elect their representatives as directors. Actually, as mentioned above, shareholders only ratify the candidates put up by management. Except in a proxy contest, there are no competing candidates.

Management uses company funds to search for new directors and to get shareholders' support for them whereas dissenting shareholders must use their own money. They do not even have access to a list of all shareholders. (The cost of obtaining such a list is prohibitive.) Thus formation of the board is actually in the hands of management.

Legally, company directors have two duties viz. duty of care and duty of loyalty. The former means that a director must exercise due diligence in making decisions and he must be able to show that he considered all reasonable alternatives before reaching a decision. Duty of loyalty means that a director has to be true to the interests of the company. This is a fiduciary duty which means that a director has to act in good faith in the best interests of the company by exercising his powers for the proper purposes for which they were conferred. This duty also requires that directors do not place themselves in a position where there is an actual or potential conflict between their duties to the company, personal interests and duties to third parties.

The board is a committee and its minimum requirements for working are a chairman and a secretary. Meetings of the board take place at regular intervals and business is transacted as per an agenda drawn up by management. A director can ask for items to be included in the agenda. The agenda and relevant information are sent to directors a few days ahead of a meeting.

All important financial statements including final accounts, cash flow statement, operating budgets, capital expenditure plans plus performance reports comparing current actuals with plans and previous year's actuals, explanations for major variations, information about share of the market, financial analysts' reports about major competitors, details of consumer preference and employee attitude surveys (if any), internal audit reports, trend analysis, important press articles on the company and competitors etc. give the information that directors find useful for preparing themselves for board meetings. The information is given to them mostly in the form of reports and sometimes by oral presentations by top managers. Plant visits and informal contacts between senior managers and directors may also take place once in a while but these are unusual.

In India, the recent Clause 49 in the listing agreement provides that the following information must be placed before the board:

1 annual operating plans, budgets and updates
2 capital budgets and updates
3 quarterly results for the company, its operating divisions and business segments
4 minutes of audit committee meetings and other board committees
5 information on recruitment and remuneration of senior officers just below the board level, including the CEO and the Company Secretary
6 show cause, demand and prosecution notices which are materially important
7 fatal or serious accidents, dangerous occurrences, any significant effluent or pollution problems

8 material default in financial obligations to and by the company or substantial non-payment for goods sold by the company

9 any issue involving possible public or product liability claims of a substantial nature and any judgement or order involving strictures on the conduct of the company or containing an adverse view that can have negative implications for the company

10 details of any joint venture or collaboration arrangement

11 transactions involving substantial payment for goodwill, brand equity or intellectual property

12 labour problems and their proposed solutions

13 materially significant sale of investments, subsidiaries, assets which are not in normal course of business

14 quarterly details of foreign exchange exposure

15 non-compliance with any regulatory, statutory or listing requirements or shareholder services such as non-payment of dividends, delay in share transfers etc.

In addition, the Naresh Chandra Committee (August 2002) wants all press releases and presentations to financial analysts made by management to be placed before the board so that the non-executive directors can know how the company is projecting itself to investors and general public.

The common problem of directors is that probably too much information is given to them. The CEO's intention might be to bury their critical judgement under the information avalanche. It requires experience, insight and judgement to quickly run through the given information and focus on underlying issues. The executive directors and CEO also have an interest in coming up with long monologues about company performance. They need to be checked in order to start a meaningful dialogue among directors. Lauenstein (1997) has observed that if a board is sufficiently large, the opportunity for an individual director to take major part in discussions can be kept nearly zero by following, what he calls, the rule of 80 and 10. Management may use at least 80 per cent of available time in a meeting for its own presentations and it should spend at least 10 minutes answering any questions raised by a director. Then a cautious manager can confine each outside director to 24 minutes per year for asking questions and getting them answered.

Board meetings last from a few to several hours, depending upon the seriousness of matters to be decided. Annual retreats of directors preferably, non-executive directors have become fashionable nowadays. During a meeting, a director has to watch out for trouble, appraise the CEO, form a judgement about the next CEO and influence strategy. Minutes of meetings are kept carefully. The company secretary is responsible for ensuring that all legal requirements for holding and conducting board meetings are complied with.

According to Mills (1981), an effective board is:

1 heterogeneous i.e. consisting of people with markedly different backgrounds and styles
2 free of non-combatants or non-contributing members
3 small
4 free of yes-men
5 task-oriented: its discussions centre on achieving specific, common objectives and not on reaching broad-brush political or policy conclusions
6 performance-oriented with regular analysis, explanation and redirection of achievement
7 flexible: its members are not bound to the boss or to a friend or to loyal subordinates. There is no permanent majority; so whichever case makes best sense is supported.
8 led democratically so each director's opinion is freely presented and impartially judged.

Chairman of the board has a duty to ensure that meetings are conducted professionally and that each member contributes to them.

Competence of a person to work as company director can be decided on the basis of the following criteria:

- **Independence:** confidence, courage, free standing posture, free thinking, avoidance of conflicts of interest.
- **Preparedness:** self-briefing, spending extra time where necessary, understanding of organization, industry, statutory and fiduciary roles, knowledge of key staff, respect for confidentiality of matters.
- **Practice as a director:** thorough homework, asking probing questions, insistence on getting all the information, participation in committees as asked, constructive participation in meetings.
- **Committee activity:** evidence of ideas, enthusiasm, constructive use of ability and influence, understanding of the process of committee work and relationship with management.
- **Contribution to organisational development:** making penetrating suggestions on innovations, strategic direction and planning, knowledge of trends and externalities, ability to win the support of outside organizations, investors, customers, suppliers etc. (Bain, Band, op. cit.)

I M Millstein insists that directors must have an understanding of the interests of all shareholders including institutional shareholders. Diversity in the perspective of individual directors is beneficial but it must be achieved without sacrificing agreement on the company's mission. Japanese boards are full of knowledgeable persons who are mostly senior executives of rival or related businesses. They have plenty of information about the work carried out by the company and their presence helps the board to ask the right questions. In the USA, however, anti-trust laws prevent appointment of such persons to the board.

Persons chosen as directors must be ready to devote the required time for discharging their responsibility. All too often, it has been found that in the name of avoiding interference in operational matters, directors abdicate their responsibility for long-term direction also. To prevent this, it is necessary to choose individuals who have the will to act when conditions require action. It is also important to appoint persons who make work stimulating for other directors and are fun to work with. Of course, directors must not go to the other extreme and start with a confrontationist stand vis-a-vis management. The board can neither be a motley collection of strong individuals nor can it be a cozy club of like-minded persons. The board chairman has to strive to ensure that independent, critical thinking is not replaced by 'groupthink' or consensual thinking.

Essentially the job of the board is to create momentum for improvement. For this purpose, it has to challenge management and create constructive tension to force it to improve its performance. The board adds value by its ability to exercise critical and independent judgement.

Independent judgement is hard to come by in our world. The Investor Responsibility Centre, USA, reports that nearly 150 directors serving on the compensation committees of Standard & Poor 500 companies in 1997 had compromised their independence through links with either a company or its CEO. It is understood that independent judgement follows from an independent position from either a company or its CEO. Therefore there exists a tangible paucity of truly independent directors. (More information on directors' independence follows.)

Election and Composition

The standard practice in India is to provide that board members retire by rotation. This facilitates continuity by providing that there will always be some continuing members on the board. These are known as staggered or classified boards in which there is no mandatory retirement age. Such boards make a good takeover defense because a quick conquest by a raider is then not possible. However, according to the studies of Securities and Exchange Commission, USA, they reduce shareholder value and go against shareholders' interest. So it has been suggested that each board should have a fixed term of 3 to 5 years and as it expires, all the members should retire simultaneously and a new board should be formed.

Composition of the board refers primarily to the combination of executive and outside directors on it. This combination and independence of the board are related. Boards are thought to become more independent as the number of outside directors increases. Outside directors represent shareholder/stakeholder/company interest while executive directors represent management and operational considerations. Board independence is highly valued in Western countries today because boards' lack of effectiveness in the recent past has arisen principally because of their dependence on management.

Executive directors are also known as inside directors and non-executive directors are called outside directors. In India, there are additional categories of whole-time, part-time directors and nominee directors. Whole-time directors should mean executive directors. Initial board-room reforms revolved around maintaining a majority of non-executive directors. Today it is emphasized that non-executive directors should be *independent* directors and their independence is getting precisely defined so as to mean no pecuniary, commercial or other connection with the concerned companies, except for the board seats. This means that full time serving and retired executives, interlocking directors i.e. companies, suppliers, customers, creditors·etc. are out of reckoning as non-executive directors. In India, the Naresh Chandra Committee has recommended that independent directors must not have more than 2% of the voting block of shares in a company which they direct.

The KM Birla Committee (2000) had earlier defined independent directors along the same lines but it did not do so in an unequivocal manner. Independent directors, it said, did not have any material pecuniary relationship with the company but the precise meaning of these terms was to be decided by each board as per its judgement. The committee rationalized its approach – its *'flexibility'*- by stating that supply of independent directors in the country was limited and a precise definition of independence would reduce it further. No wonder, this approach drew a lot of flak and critics pointed out that this happened because of the dominance of promoters in the committee. The committee – its chairman is himself a big promoter – wanted to make all the right sounding gestures without disturbing the status quo. The Naresh Chandra Committee ridiculed the above approach by calling it a piece of circular, tautological reasoning. The Naresh Chandra Committee was appointed by the ministry of finance of the Government of India and it consisted of senior bureaucrats.

The Naresh Chandra Committee defined independence of directors in the following manner.

An independent director of a company is a non-executive director who:

1   apart from receiving director's remuneration, does not have any material pecuniary relationships or transactions with the company, its promoters, its senior management or its holding company, its subsidiaries and associated companies

2   is not related to promoters or management at the board level or one level below the board (relations include spouse and dependent parents, children and siblings)

3   has not been an executive of the company in the last three years

4   is not a partner or an executive of the statutory auditor firm, the internal audit firm that are associated with the company and has not been a partner or executive of any such firm in the last three years; this also applies to legal and consulting firms that have a material association with the company

5   is not a significant supplier, vendor or customer of the company

6   is not a substantial shareholder of the company i.e. does not own more than 2% of the block of voting shares

7   has not been a director-independent or otherwise-of the company for more than three terms of three years each.

The Cadbury Committee is also on record that stock option plans to directors would go against the requirement of their independence. (Opinions differ on this point. Others have suggested that directors should also be shareholders of their companies to make them act responsibly. With this logic, the greater the shareholding, greater will be the diligence by directors.)

Inclusion of independent, outside directors on the board tends to strengthen internal control mechanism and to reduce the possibility of directors acting in collusion against shareholders interest. The number of independent directors in American boards has been rising steadily but now it is realized that this independence in itself, does not guarantee good governance. Independent, disinterested directors may turn out to be simply *uninterested* directors. Therefore the suggestion (Monks and Minow, 1995) that directors' ownership interest in a company must be significant in terms of their own, personal wealth and then they will be serious about discharging their duties.

Financial markets generally regard the appointment of outside directors as the right step in monitoring management. Empirical evidence on the contribution of non-executive directors to governance is not conclusive. Noe and Rebello (1996) have found that slight majority of outside directors is better than domination of either inside or outside directors. Some studies have found that stock prices go up when outside directors are added to the board. The study by Weisbach (1998) concluded that firms with outside directors-dominated boards, were more likely than inside director-dominated board companies to remove the CEO for under-performance. (CEO turnover has been treated as an important indicator of board effectiveness in concerned studies.) Weisbach's study also found that the response of stock performance to the decision to remove CEO was three times larger for outsider-dominated boards than insider-dominated boards.

Hermalin and Weisbach, in their study based on a sample of 142 firms in the USA (1998) found that:

a   higher proportions of outside directors are not associated with superior firm performance but are associated with better decisions concerning such issues as acquisitions, executive compensation and CEO turnover

b   board size is negatively related to both general firm performance and quality of decision-making

c   poor firm performance, CEO turnover and changes in ownership structure are often associated with changes in the membership of the board.

In India, Kathuria and Dash studied CMIE data for 1994 with respect to about 400 companies and found that size of board significantly affected *board* performance and increase in board size led to improved company performance upto a point.

There are other studies which have found no relationship between board composition and firm performance. At least one study points out the limit to board independence. This study by Murthy (1998) was based on the performance of some Australian companies between 1992 and 1994. It found that the more independent the board, the lower the returns to shareholders and also lower the level of sales growth. Conversely, smaller, more cohesive and supportive boards were associated with better company performance. Empirical evidence on this score is, in short, mixed and tentative.

Current preoccupation with non-executive directors has led to a neglect of the role of executive directors and their place on the board has now been eclipsed. It is thought that they cannot be influential board members in their own right because they have to vote with the CEO-cum-Executive Director. However, their inclusion on the board serves the following important purposes:

1   The CEO-Director is forced to concentrate on team-building instead of getting on with the right of command.
2   The CEO-Director's monopoly on information and interpretation of strategic development is broken.
3   Outside directors get a regular opportunity to evaluate leading contenders in the board meeting. This helps succession planning.
4   Inside directors provide useful information and new insights. These are particularly important in boards which require technical sophistication but cannot appoint knowledgeable outsiders because of conflicts of interest and anti-monopoly laws.
5   Election to the board is an acknowledgement of the importance of particular executives and so is a major motivator. Prospects of directorship secure executives' loyalty and they are less tempted by outside offers. (Bowen, 1994)

Size of the Board

Some empirical observations about size of the board and firms' performance have already been made. They posit a weak, inverse relationship between the two. So smaller boards ought to be preferred. However, if large boards make individual directors anonymous and dilute their accountability then smaller boards fail to reach sufficient diversity in terms of background, experience and perspective. There is general agreement that reducing board size is against shareholder interest. During the takeover tide of mid-1980s in the USA, many companies had tried to reduce the size of the board to make boards cohesive for fending off hostile bids. On the basis of this experience, experts have concluded that changing the size without seeking shareholders' approval is inimical to their interest. A range of 10 to 15 members is acceptable to many. Blair has stated that 10 should be the maximum strength of any board. The Naresh Chandra Committee has recommended a minimum board size of 7 members. A study by Spencerstuart, an executive search firm, has found that the average board size of 100 largest boards in the USA had declined from 15 in 1988 to 13 or less in 1993.

Board Chairman

Many companies used to follow the practice of appointing their CEOs as board chairman also. The argument was – an organization had to be finally led by one person and if these positions were filled by separate persons, either the chairman would become a rubber-stamp or he would usurp the role of CEO. This practice has been widely criticized because it tilts the scales in favour of management and reduces its accountability to the board as it obstructs the board from holding management accountable for the use of its vast power.

The Cadbury Committee made a strong case for separating the two roles for preserving board's independence. This recommendation did not find favour with the Hampel Committee (1998) which felt that it would lead to unnecessary expense and wastage.

Many companies in the UK have implemented this recommendation of the Cadbury Committee and today only about one-third of the largest companies in the UK have a joint CEO-Board Chairman. In contrast, a majority of American companies have CEOs who are also the chairman of the board. One study by Rechner and Dalton (1991) found that companies with separate roles of the CEO and the board chairman consistently outperformed those which combined these roles. Yet, a widespread view in the USA is that their separation does not achieve much.

In India, the KM Birla Committee (2000) has linked this issue with board composition. It provides that if a board has non-executive chairman, at least one-third of the board should comprise independent directors and in case of an executive chairman, at least one-half of the board should consist of independent directors. Otherwise, it has been a non-issue in India so far.

Term of Office

As long as staggered boards remain, retirement of individual members of the board is an important issue. Once appointed, directors must be able to complete one term to office. They can be truly independent only when they know for sure that the chairman would not oust them through no-confidence motions before the agreed time.

It is necessary to consider the retirement age of directors seriously. In India, directorships have been considered a sinecure and through reappointments directors like to continue to hold office till eventually death intervenes. So the idea of retirement is difficult to digest for many people. (One of the reasons for the clash between Russi Modi and Ratan Tata in the board of Tata Sons was that the latter wanted to introduce mandatory retirement at the age of 75 years for the directors.) However, retirement age should be clearly specified to build up a cadre of professionals to work as directors. This move will help companies to introduce fresh blood, new ideas and outlook in their boards.

The other side of this issue is that a company might stand to lose contributions of veterans who have developed deep insights into the working of a company. This might appear to be a trivial point but in the USA, Intel Corporation's corporate governance guidelines state flatly that the company does not believe in fixed terms of office for directors as it would then stand the risk of losing experienced directors. The guidelines state further that the company would rather make some other arrangement for injecting fresh ideas and viewpoints into the board.

Compensation of Directors

Directors receive sitting fees for the meetings they attend and also some perquisites which vary from company to company. In the USA, prior to the takeover era, many powerful CEOs followed a deliberate policy of conferring lavish benefits upon directors in order to get their concurrence. The practice invited a lot of criticism and suspicion of shareholders. Still, directors in the USA are more lavishly paid as compared to those in other countries. In 1995, the average annual total compensation of a director in the USA was $ 55000, in Germany $ 30000 and in the UK $ 25000. In India, executive directors (managing and whole-time directors) usually receive a commission based on profit and this makes their compensation generous. Bare sitting fees are however, considered inadequate at Rs. 5000 per meeting, particularly in the light of new responsibilities being thrust upon directors and it is felt that if leading professionals are to be attracted to this field, sitting fees should move up.

In the USA, stock options form a part of executive directors' compensation in many cases. It is suggested that these options should be restricted options i.e. the concerned director should get a right to sell these shares only after say, 12 to 36 months from his retirement from the board. Otherwise, it is feared that directors could encourage a short-term increase in share price at the cost of long-term business viability. Another problem is that this practice can encourage insider trading. In the USA, rules against insider trading are strictly enforced by stock exchange authorities. Also it has strong markets and the spirit of competition is irrepressible. Therefore stock options to directors may not be problematic. In India, with her underdeveloped markets and with the track record of her business promoters, they will *create* more problems rather than solve the existing ones.

Board Committees

Boards have limited time at their disposal for meetings. So committees are popularly formed to consider certain matters in depth. These committees are also used to consider *confidential* matters. Almost any subject within the board's authority can be delegated to a committee but the board has to take full responsibility for its actions and also retain full decision-making process within the board.

The advantages and disadvantages of board committees are set out below:

Advantages:
- allow time to focus on a specific issue
- build up more specialized activity and capability in the board
- reduce burden on board meetings
- assist decision-making by providing more time and focus
- may avoid disagreement on the main board
- are useful for sensitive confidential matters
- allow non-executive directors to operate in a supervisory role, away from executive directors but under the board's control.

Disadvantages:
- more time is needed as committee attendance is in addition to board attendance
- increase reporting and coordination tasks
- may distance committee activities from board activities.

Experienced board chairman advise that careful cost-benefit analysis should be made before setting up any committee. (John Harper, 2000)

Instead of going for two-tier boards, the Anglo-American companies have preferred to form different board committees. In the 1960s and the 1970s, salary and bonus committee, finance committee and executive committee could be found in American boards. Now audit committees have become mandatory in the USA as well as India and apart from them, nomination or succession and remuneration or compensation committees are also seen. These various committees are classified by some as productivity and monitoring committees.

In 1972, Arthur Goldberg, a retired judge of the US Supreme Court resigned in less than two years after joining the TWA board. He had tried to create a committee of outside directors to supervise the effectiveness of management and also the board. He also proposed that a small support-cum-technical staff be created to report only to the board. He wanted persons with a background in economics, law and science to serve on the staff which would review management reports. He thought this would remove the anomaly of directors' 'independent' judgement being based on information supplied by management. Both the ideas were new (and threatening!) at the time, managers and directors alike opposed them and Goldberg quit his directorship.

Much change has taken place in boardrooms since then. In 1978, the New York Stock Exchange made audit committees of outside directors compulsory on the boards of all listed companies. The Cadbury Committee was a major supporter of audit committees and indeed, it gave a major role to board committees to reform boardroom practices. The KM Birla Committee on corporate governance caused Clause 49 to be added to the listing agreement in India and one of its provisions is compulsory formation of audit committees in all listed companies. Independent directors are given the main responsibility of work in board committees. The idea of a board secretariat is yet to find similar acceptance because such a permanent structure would probably be found very intrusive.

Audit Committee

According to the Cadbury Committee, this Committee would work to ratify the selection of external auditor, to check the adequacy of internal controls and to ensure that published financial statements were not misleading. These remain the basic terms of reference of this committee. In addition, it is also being pressed into service in new areas such as compliance with regulations, review of corporate ethics code, preparation of management discussion and analysis section in the annual report, tax and accounting impact of executive compensation etc. Independent non-executive directors are members of this committee. It is broadly expected to be an additional, top-level oversight mechanism to function between a business's accounting and internal audit functions and its external auditors.

Nomination Committee

Through this committee, the Board of Directors participate in deciding board composition. It is concerned with issues such as size of the board, qualifications for directorship, selection process, balance between executive directors and non-executive directors, retirement age of members etc. It has to ensure that current members *continue* to remain eligible for various assignments. By reviewing candidates considered for nomination, this committee has to ensure that the board chairman does not exercise patronage in selecting the board. If this committee functions effectively, it can go a long way in ensuring that outsiders see the board as a well-functioning monitoring tool. At present, however, it remains a poor relation of audit committee.

Remuneration/Compensation Committee

It is entrusted with the task of determining the compensation of the CEO, other top executives and executive-directors. Their compensation is an important motivator to these ambitious, highly competitive persons. At the same time, the desire of executives to reward themselves excessively has been one of the major factors behind the launch of the corporate governance movement. Charkham and Simpson (1998) have pointed out that very high compensation along with a lot of power and media exposure have created an unprecedented tilt in favour of company executives in the twentieth century. Previously positions of power were filled by people who had a sense of public duty and these positions were themselves thought to be a reward. Hence meagre financial compensation used to be attached to them. Now company executives, in their zest for feathering their own nests, have reversed the trend and ushered in an era of selfishness.

The compensation package of top managers and executive-directors is likely to consist of many components such as bonus, commission, stock options, other perquisites etc. These parts need to be combined in an imaginative fashion and the whole package must be related to performance and it must be competitive. The Compensation Committee must provide for disclosure of top management pay in the annual report.

Evaluation of Board Performance

Hostile takeovers can be said to provide a final evaluation of a board of directors but they cannot take the place of a regular, systematic review by the board itself of its processes and performance. The board chairman must evaluate the performance of individual members and also of the board as a whole. The criteria for such an evaluation will be clear from the following extract:

Ideal Board

1	Composition	– Items reserved for board
		– Formal appraisal of working
		– Sufficient number of meetings
		– Occasional meetings of non-executive directors with the CEO
2	Governance	– Terms of reference
		– Primacy of shareholder interest
		– Audit committee's interaction with external auditors
3	Board agenda	– Well-documented, timely
		– Sufficient, concise information
		– Covers key areas, strategic and management development items
		– Gives sufficient time
4	Non-executive Directors	– Independently selected
		– Appropriately rewarded
		– Fixed tenure with probability of renewal
		– Serious about discharging their responsibilities
5	Relations with Management	– Appropriate incentives
		– Succession plans
6	Communication	– Review investor relations programme
		– Best practice in disclosure
7	Culture	– Openness
		– Chairman and CEO separate
		– Minimum 3 non-executive directors

(Adapted from Bain, Band, op. cit. p.45)

Another rather revolutionary prescription for a model Board of Directors is as follows:

- all directors are elected for one year term
- at least 2/3rd of the directors are independent
- no director is more than 72 years of age
- there is an independent lead director and
- outside directors meet alone at least once a year. (Colvin, 1999)

Some Suggestions for Improvement

Michael Porter headed a research project – 'capital choices' – in the early 1990s. A major concern of the project was the adverse effects of short-termism on corporate performance. To remove them, Porter suggested that:

a capital gains tax scheme should be altered to persuade investors to hold stock options for minimum 5 years

b long-term institutional holders of a company's equity should be given data on a wider range of performance indicators

c managers must be told to exercise their stock options after a minimum lock-in period.

As regards board working, Porter suggested that large, long-term institutional shareholders should be given board representation and boards should include important customers, suppliers, financial advisors, employees and community representatives.

With the ascendancy of market-control perspective, these recommendations have been gathering dust but they certainly led to a lot of discussion. Then some more radical suggestions were made by Bavly in 1999. His proposals are:

a an independent, outside body similar to a stock exchange should appoint and also pay all independent, outside directors of companies.

b board size should be restricted to maximum 6 persons.

c tenure of directors should be restricted to 3 or at the most 5 years.

Allan Kennedy (2000) has made the following recommendations for improving board working.

a All existing CEOs of large public companies should be banned from serving on the boards of other large public companies.

b There should be stringent rules regarding dereliction of duty by directors. For instance, a director should be removed from his post if he fails to attend 2 board meetings consecutively.

c An independent body should be set up to prescribe standards and rules of conduct for directors.

d A board should have 5 or 6 members and 2 or 3 of them should represent outside constituencies that are important to a company. The number of inside or executive directors must not exceed 2 and they should be non-voting members of the board.

e Each board should have a secretariat working for it.

f Boards should be given explicit responsibility to develop targets for long-term viability of business.

g Every board should have a standing stakeholder committee. Its duty will be to monitor the effect of company actions on each stakeholder group.

h Each board should report annually to shareholders about the specific actions it is taking to build long-term future of the company. The report should spell out how the company expects to create sustainable competitive advantage.

i   Any long-term contract entered into with major stakeholders of the company should be disclosed to the shareholders.

j   An outside agency should be appointed to conduct audit of overall board performance and performance of individual directors.

Other important suggestions which are being tried out are as follows:

1   **Pool of independent directors:** A ready pool of competent individuals to work as independent directors is going to be a necessity in future. In due course of time, the work of directing business will be professionalized. Institutional investors can play an important role in developing a cadre of directors who will work on five or six boards at the most. The National Association of Corporate' Directors (NACD), Washington and Promotion of Non-executive Directors (PRO NED) established in the UK in 1981 under the chairmanship or Sir Adrian Cadbury have taken a lead in this regard. NACD operates as a trade association and it provides study courses, hosts conferences, carries out research and publishes a magazine – **Director's Monthly**. It convenes working groups on topics such as executive compensation, the CEO and director evaluation etc. It also maintains a database on candidates for directorships and carries out board evaluations.

      PRO NED works as a head-hunting firm and provides boards with qualified non-executive directors. It maintains a register of names of actual or potential outside directors who have wide experience and suitable qualifications for the job. It advises companies on the suitability of particular appointments. It undertakes appropriate publicity measures for greater use of outside directors. It has also formulated guidelines to outside directors to discharge their duties. It contributes, from time to time, to current thinking on board structures and role of outside directors.

2   **Lead directors:** One suggestion has called for creating a slot for a lead director who would be an outside director and who would be consulted by the board chairman on matters such as: selection of members of different board committees, agendas of meetings, their effectiveness, adequacy of information provided to directors etc. The lead director is to play a pivotal role in evaluating CEOs. He should combine the assessments of the CEO's performance by individual directors and pass them on to the CEO in confidence. General Motor's board guidelines on significant corporate governance issues (1994) include this provision.

      Some Canadian companies follow a variant to this practice in 'designated directors'. An outside director meeting certain criteria, is designated for a period of upto 3 years, for carrying out specified work such as communicating with shareholders, working out special compensation rights etc.

3   **Quinquennial Election:** Martin Lipton has suggested that shareholders should elect the entire board only once every five years. At these elections, shareholders with some minimum holding should have access to the proxy machinery to nominate their own candidates and they should be allowed to

comment on management's performance. If the company has not met its goals, the incumbent board would lose its position. Lipton has also proposed that outside directors should serve on only three board at a time but draw higher remuneration from each.

4   **Annual session:** It is suggested that an annual meeting of only non-executive directors will be useful for performance appraisal of the CEO.

5   **Peer review:** In British Airways, every director submits a peer group review once in three years. It is highly useful for evaluation of the performance of the entire board, too.

6   **Greater role for nomination committees:** Some experts want directors to suggest more names for choosing other board members. They feel that shareholders should also do so but the CEO is best kept out of this committee.

7   **Greater accountability to shareholders:** To ensure this, individual directors' votes on key corporate resolutions should be recorded in proxy statements. This will help improve the quality of boardroom debate and directors will then have an incentive to engage in a debate on vital matters. It is further suggested that the data of votes cast on different resolutions should be made available to shareholders' organizations for preparing **'director scorecards'**. They in conjunction with self-evaluation sheets will help in evaluation of board performance. This system will help directors to push back proposals for higher executive pay, staggered boards etc. which are likely to emanate from management.

8   **Own funding:** The board should not be dependent on information provided by management if it wants to develop its independent perspective on any issue. So it should have some own funds at its disposal so as to get information, hire consultants and researchers etc.

9   **Focus on long-run:** To secure it, several suggestions have been made. They include a tax on stock trades, tax rebates for long-term stock holdings and elimination of quarterly reporting.

10 **Qualifications of directors:** It is suggested that in the interest of getting bright, competent persons as directors and in making directorship a profession, higher qualifications and standards must be set for working directors. These standards should emphasize greater diversity of experience. Simultaneously, clear tenure limits should also be specified for directors.

11 **Board secretariat:** To enable the board to function independently, it has been recommended that there should be a dedicated staff of 20 to 30 qualified persons for every board. This staff will maintain board-specific reporting system and conduct special investigations as requested by individual directors.

Indian Boards

The entire discussion of corporate governance reforms in the West has taken place in the context of strong CEOs, weak boards and fragmented, weak shareholders. Much abuse of power was made by executives in these conditions and then shareholders started urging directors to play a more active, even interventionist role.

Indian businesses operate in a different environment where CEOs are simply not strong enough. Until recently, Indian boards too, have been rubber-stamp bodies but in following the policy of passive concurrence, their loyalty has firmly been with promoters and inside directors rather than managers. Indian directors have all along been representatives of promoters and promoter families.

A chief feature of the Indian board of directors is plurality of directorships i.e. one person holding directorships in a number of companies. Domination of a few business and managing agency houses and shortage of qualified persons had brought this situation about earlier. More particularly, during the Second World War and immediately afterwards, Indian business houses promoted a large number of new companies and multiple directorships came into existence. Therefore the Bhabha Committee (1953–54) recommended as upper limit of 20 directorships which was incorporated in the Companies Act, 1956. Nigam and Joshi's study of 1502 directors in 1963 showed that 73 per cent of them were plural directors.

All the boards in India are staggered boards and directors take turns in retiring. This is known as retiring by rotation. Most of the directors seek re-election and manage to get re-elected.

Another feature that stands out in case of the Indian boards, is the presence of nominee directors. Public financial institutions have been appointing them since 1971. In case of large borrowers, nominee directors were thought necessary to curb the exuberance of promoters and to make the voice of minority shareholders and public (the money lent by these institutions came from state exchequer) heard in the board-rooms. Nominee directors have not been able to discharge this onerous responsibility but because of their induction, at least preliminary formalities such as sending notices and agenda of meetings in advance, furnishing performance reports, annual budgets etc. started getting completed in large companies.

Gupta obtained the following results from his study of boards in 444 listed companies in 1982–83:

1   They had, on average, more compact size-range i.e. 6.5 to 11.5 members – as compared to American, British and Japanese boards.
2   There was an overwhelming tilt in favour on non-executives in board composition. Small companies mostly had no or at the most only one executive director on their boards. In no case was a team of professional managers as executive directors found on the board. ('Independent' non-executive directors was however, a very remote matter.)
3   A majority of surveyed companies had separate positions of the board chairman and the CEO. The Board Chairmen were mostly non-executive chairmen with clear connection with dominant family owners.

If the above are considered as positive features then on the negative side were

these:
1 A majority of companies had just about four to six meetings in a year.
2 Board committees were not popular. At the most, a share transfer committee and a management/executive committee could be found. Audit committees were unheard of.

Gupta's overall conclusion in this study was that the Indian companies were by and large, dominated by one man or one family and they exhibited a great unwillingness to share authority in the real sense with a professional team. Gupta attributed this tendency to the feudal ethos in the Indian society.

Nominee Directors

The Dutt Committee (1969) had stated that financial institutions should participate in directing business in public interest and for countering concentration of economic power. So it mooted the idea of nominee directors who would act as agents of change, in liberating boards from the domination of controlling groups. Public financial institutions had started giving loan finance to businesses at concessional rates after 1969 when major commercial banks were nationalized. So in 1971 a mandatory provision for appointing nominee directors was made in the loan agreements of these bodies. In case of very large loans, it was provided that nominee directors would be compulsorily appointed on the boards of borrowing companies and public financial institutions were given an option to convert 20% of their assistance above a certain limit into equity. (This was the famous convertibility clause.) The number of nominee directors was not specified and the institutions enjoyed flexibility on this score.

In the changed circumstances since 1991 when financial liberalization began, the convertibility clause was dropped and appointment of nominee directors ceased to be mandatory. SEBI has supported this change and has advised public financial institutions to use the instrument of nominee directors sparingly, on a selective basis. So public financial institutions now look at it as an enabling provision to be used to safeguard their commercial interests. This change, inter alia, is a reflection of the transition of the Indian financial system. In a sense, this is ironical as in the UK and the USA, institutional investors are being asked to take more active interest in the governance of investee companies and we in India are moving in the opposite direction.

The decision to appoint nominee directors compulsorily on the boards of large borrowers was a political decision. It was made because loans were given to businesses at a concessional rates of interest. Public financial institutions did not themselves ask for this measure nor were commercial considerations involved in it.

The convertibility clause came in for bitter criticism from businesses from day one. Nominee directors did not evoke such a sharp reaction but these two points became an emotive issue. Over the years, public financial institutions came to possess shares of borrowing companies on the basis of the convertibility clause. However, these were a small lot compared to the shares picked up by these institutions in underwriting agreements (Patil, 2001). They did not hold on to these shares but sold them in the market after studying current trends. This was done in such a manner that existing good managements were not disturbed nor was cornering by a few parties possible. As soon as borrowing companies repaid their loans fully, nominee directors were withdrawn from their boards. In the first place, they jointly appointed two nominee directors only on the board of any company. In short, public financial institutions acted in a thoroughly professional manner in this respect.

Criticism by business promoters was understandable because they treat businesses as their family property in spite of shareholding that ranged from 15 to 30 per cent or even less. They *are* used to boards with convenient people such as fellow industrialists with whom understanding about non-interference is reached well in advance and professionals who are awarded some consultancy agreements. So the common situation is that directors even before they come to a meeting are already agreed on not raising inconvenient issues.

Under these circumstances, nominee directors found that their path toward the avowed goals of furthering public interest and countering concentration of economic power was strewn with obstacles. This plus the political games of promoters put public financial institutions on the defensive.

Gupta tried to find out the reasons for the overall ineffectiveness of nominee directors by contacting 400 of them in 1982. One hundred and ninety-one (191) directors responded to his queries and a majority of them (63 per cent) emphasized their advisory role i.e. providing professional advice to CEO rather than the control role of guarding against managerial abuse and ensuring social responsibility. So nominee directors themselves were not prepared for the role that had been foreseen for them.

It must be admitted that the role of a nominee director is an unenviable one. He has to don two hats – he has to protect the interests of his institution and also those of public shareholders in the face of passive resistance of promoters. The nominee directors were all senior professional managers in the public sector; they were not persons with any background of family business. They found the going tough. Nominee directors face conflict of interest since as lenders and as shareholders their interests are different. Even as shareholders, the role of relational, long-term investees was expected of public financial institutions. (See Chapter 7.)

Shareholding of public financial institutions (IFCI, IDBI, ICICI) in the Indian companies was not large. LIC, GIC and UTI had larger holdings. Of course, as major or the biggest lenders, public financial institutions had a lot of indirect influence. Again, the Gupta's study (1981–83) of shareholding pattern of 365 companies listed on the Calcutta Stock Exchange found that except in those cases where they were majority shareholders, their controlling power was indeterminate.

They had to act in unison for taking decisive steps. Controlling power in a company depended upon factors such as distribution of equity, whether there were two groups contesting for control or whether tussle was between public financial institutions and existing dominant owners. Public confidence enjoyed by different promoter groups was also an important factor. Public financial institutions commonly found that other holders usually ganged up against them and did their utmost to protect incubent management. Ironically, even public sympathy did not always favour the institutions.

One persistent criticism of the practice of appointing nominee directors is that it encourages insider trading. Nominee directors come to know about operational performance and problems of business before the information reaches the market. Since public financial institutions participate in secondary capital market regularly, they can use this early information to their advantage in buying/selling shares. This has the effect of security prices being rigged and small shareholders, not being privy to such inside information are the losers.

This is a valid point and to avoid this charge, institutions have to build an arms-length relationship between nominee directors and their investment/portfolio departments. In fact, this must be a structural requirement in case of all institutional shareholders.

In India, insider trading is practised widely but proving the charge in a court of law has been very difficult. Therefore there have been very few convictions on this point. All the business families and promoters in the country indulge in insider trading. Almost all business groups have their investment/finance companies and they trade actively in the securities of group companies on the basis of insider information. Promoters have had access to far more inside information as compared to nominee directors but promoters have effectively used this point in their propaganda against public financial institutions.

Judged against this backdrop, it is small wonder that nominee directors have not been able to live up to the lofty dreams of the Dutt Committee. However, their appointment to company boards was a bold step and there is a continuing need for nominee directors as long as business management is not professionalised; as long as promoters ignore the rights of minority shareholders and do not follow good corporate governance practices. Therefore public financial institutions should continue to use this measure. They should use it selectively to safeguard their commercial interests. They should also use this measure in such a manner that appointment of nominee directors becomes akin to whistle-blowing: their appointment should send a signal to the public that all is *not* well with the business.

Current Changes

It will be exaggeration to say that winds of change are cutting through Indian boardrooms and are clearing away cobwebs of obsolete practices. However, some zephyrs can definitely be felt. Mandatory provisions of the KM Birla Committee and continual improvements in international practices have brought about change and in many companies, boards are getting down to work. Companies such as Infosys, the ICICI Bank, Dr Reddy's Laboratories, Godrej Consumer Products, Asian Paints, Marico, Orchid Chemicals and Pharmaceuticals etc. show determination to improve the working of their boards. They are inviting independent, informed persons such as business strategists, business school professors on their boards and are listening to them. Before inviting such persons they have planned the structure of their boards. With structure coming first, the role a director is to play and his responsiblity are given primary importance. Dr Reddy's Laboratories has created a scientific advisory board to induct knowledgeable persons as directors.

After getting the right persons, these companies are introducing necessary processes so that these persons do in fact, contribute to better performance. Some companies have introduced peer group reviews. Regular reviews of contributions of whole boards as well as individual directors have also begun. Steps are also taken to create an open, democratic culture where dissent is not only tolerated but is encouraged.

- In Polaris, directors participate along with employees in the annual goal-setting round.
- ICICI bank insists that middle managers regularly make presentations to the board.
- The transformation of Infosys from a services company to a consultancy firm as also its entry into business process outsourcing was initiated by its board.
- Godrej Consumer Products consulted Confederation of Indian Industry for forming its board. It advised it to choose independent professionals and not industrialists. The company agreed and the new directors promptly suggested a reorganization of business along product lines.
- Merger of the ICICI and the ICICI Bank was worked out with active help from the ICICI board. Independent directors of the ICICI Bank feel that the bank, in concentrating on its NPAs (non performing assets), has become risk-averse and is only looking at a small number of large, creditworthy accounts. They want it to move down to small and medium enterprises also.
- In case of Polaris Software Lab, its board forced Arun Jain – Chairman and Managing Director – to give up his idea of acquiring other business at the peak of dotcom boom.
- The board of Orchid Chemicals asked its Managing Director to get his growth plan reviewed by McKinsey and Company and it was accepted only after necessary changes were made in it.

The cynical view about the above developments is that of superficial tinkering to create an impression that serious restructuring is afoot. Critics feel that most of the Indian businesses want to avoid the hard work involved in restructuring; they do not have the required vision and capacity and so the cosmetic changes in board composition cannot go far. Thus it is argued that a company like Godrej Consumer Products does not create value for its shareholders and so changes in its board do not lead to any improvement in it profitability/ stock price. Infosys, Dr Reddy's Laboratories, Hindalco and a handful of other Indian companies are exceptions to the above generalization.

Appendix

Kumar Mangalam Birla Committee on Corporate Governance

The Securities and Exchange Board of India (SEBI) formed a committee in 1999 to promote and raise the standard of corporate governance in listed companies in India. Mr KM Birla headed this committee and it is known by his name. SEBI accepted the recommendations of this committee in January 2000 and to implement them, a new clause – Clause 49 – was inserted into the listing agreement for new companies. For existing companies, a phased schedule for compliance till March 2003 was announced and implemented.

The committee's report discusses corporate governance under the following main headings:
1   Board of Directors
2   Audit Committee
3   Remuneration of Directors
4   Board Procedures
5   Management
6   Shareholders
7   Report on Corporate Governance and
8   Compliance

In addition to specific mandatory prescriptions in the above eight areas, the committee has also listed the following non-mandatory requirements:
a   All companies should set up remuneration committees of Board of Directors.
b   The half-yearly declarations of financial performance should be sent to each household of shareholders.
c   A non-executive chairman of the board should be entitled to maintain his/her office at company expense.
d   To make corporate democracy real, shareholders who are unable to attend general meetings should be able to vote by postal ballot so far as key decisions are concerned.

Committee's main recommendations are summarized below:

A *Board of Directors*
1   Not less than 50 per cent of the board would comprise non-executive directors. The number of independent directors would depend upon whether the chairman is an executive or non-executive. In the case of a non-executive chairman, at least one-third of the board should comprise independent directors and in the case of an executive chairman, at least one-half of the board should comprise independent directors.
    (Independent directors are directors who, apart from their directors' remuneration, do not have any material pecuniary relationship or transactions with the company.)

2 All pecuniary relationships or transactions of non-executive directors with the company should be disclosed in the annual report.

B *Audit Committee*

1 It will consist of minimum 3 non-executive directors and majority of them will be independent. The chairman of the committee shall be an independent director. He will attend the AGM to answer shareholders' queries.
2 The audit committee will meet at least thrice a year.
3 Role of the audit committee will include, inter alia, matters such as appointment/removal of external auditors, oversight of financial reporting system, review of financial statements, discussions with internal auditors etc.

C *Remuneration of Directors*

1 Board of Directors shall decide remuneration of non-executive directors.
2 In the annual report's corporate governance section, the following disclosure on details of directors' remuneration will be made:
   - remuneration package of all directors
   - fixed portion of remuneration and performance-linked incentives
   - service contracts, notice period and severance fees
   - stock options, if any.

D *Board Procedures*

1 Board meetings will be held at least 4 times in a year. (Minimum information to be given to the board for a meeting is given in detail.)
2 A director shall not be a member in more than 10 committees or act as chairman of more than 5 committees across all companies in which he is a director.
   Under the remaining headings, the committee's main recommendations are:
   a. A management discussion and analysis report should form a part of the annual report to shareholders. This report will include discussion on the following points, within limits set by a company's competitive position:
      - industry structure and developments
      - opportunities and threats
      - segment wise or product wise performance
      - outlook
      - risks and concerns
      - internal control systems and their adequacy
      - financial performance with respect to operational matters
      - material developments in human resource industrial relations front including number of persons employed.
   b. Shareholders'/investors' grievance committee to be formed.
   c. In the annual report of the company, there will be a separate section on corporate governance. (Suggested list of items to be given in the section

is separately indicated.) Non-compliance with any mandatory requirement will be highlighted there.

d. Statutory auditors of the company shall give a compliance certificate regarding conditions of corporate governance. This certificate will be sent, along with annual returns, to the stock exchange.

7

Institutional Investors: Much Ado About Nothing?

A debate about the role of institutional investors was a major part of the corporate governance controversy of the 1990s. Steadily since the late 1950s in the UK, the percentage of institutional investors, ownership in the corporate sector has increased and at present institutional investors are the single largest block holders in the economy. The USA has followed in the footsteps of the UK in this respect. Given their large presence, it was felt that institutional investors were ideally placed to overcome the problem of shareholder apathy or powerlessness. A strong, activist role by institutional investors was therefore advocated. At the same time, it was also felt that institutional investors were behind the stability of German – Japanese corporate governance systems and so the appealing idea of relational investment could be practised through them. Thus Cadbury Committee asked institutional investors to look upon voting rights as an asset and to use them in monitoring and improving efficiency of portfolio companies.

Among the three dominant perspectives on corporate governance viz. organization-control, capital market-control and stakeholder-control perspectives, the first two take diametrically opposite positions on causes of the governance problem and the role of capital market. According to organization-control perspective, threat of takeovers and recourse to high dividend payout to avoid them have been responsible for diverting managers' attention from organizational investment and learning in the long run. This is thought to be reflected in the declining competitive position of the American industry. In other words, capital market is the root cause of the problem. Capital market-control perspective concentrates on agency costs and the divergence of interest of shareholders and managers. It lauds the role of capital market in forcing managers to part with excess surplus and to hand it over to shareholders. With this controversy about the role of capital market, the alternate arrangement of close, internal monitoring by institutional investors appeared to be alluring.

The Issue

Matters however, are more complicated. In fact, as it turns out, the odds are heavily against an interventionist role by institutional investors. The advantages and disadvantages of institutional investors oversight have been summarized in Table 7.1.

Table 7.1. *Effect of corporate monitoring by institutional investors*

Advantages	Disadvantages
1 Reduction in agency costs	1 Practical difficulties: a institutional investors not keen on activism
2 Efficient monitoring: institutional investors are better informed about market developments, have trained research analysts and so can monitor corporates more efficiently as compared to individual shareholders.	b conflict of interest for institutional investors, representatives c investment strategies rely heavily on capital market and so cannot be thought of as alternate mechanism to it d political constraints e institutional investors can raise issues of fairness but cannot improve performance f who will guard the guardians? g free riding or collective action problem
3 Relational investment and providing support to implement long-term investment projects and to take risk.	2 Insider trading 3 Creation of monopoly through coming together of industrial and finance capital

These points need careful consideration before one can arrive at a reasonable conclusion regarding superiority of monitoring by institutional investors as a mechanism of corporate oversight. However first one must know who exactly these institutional investors are, how they work, what constraints they face and how they can intervene to improve governance of portfolio companies.

Among institutional investors, mutual funds and unit trusts fall in one category and the rest viz. insurance companies, pension funds, trusts and endowments etc. fall in the other. Mutual funds receive and pay out funds on a day-to-day basis in their open-ended schemes. So instead of developing a long-term investment perspective, they find it convenient to make use of the stock market price index. Even for their close-ended schemes, they may use investment strategies of indexing and active investing. Competition among mutual funds steers them away from relational investment which requires commitment of time and trust-based consultation with investee companies. (It will be fruitful to distinguish between portfolio and investee companies at this juncture. An institutional investor invests in a portfolio company with a view to earning short-term returns while it has long-term interests in an investee company. Also recall the distinction – owner investors and portfolio investors in Chapter 4.)

Institutional investors in the second category receive investible funds for a long time. Life insurance companies and pension funds have a set, fairly certain payout and so they can commit their funds in a particular avenue. Because of the size of their holdings, it is frequently difficult for them to quietly liquidate their holdings in the market. So they can go for relational investment and have an active interest in the governance of investee companies.

However, there exist many legal restrictions which have been designed to create an arm's length relationship between financiers and industrial concerns. This distance between finance and industrial capital is a basic feature of the Anglo-American financial system. These legal provisions are summarized in Table 7.2. They will make it clear that prohibition of insider trading and formation of monopolies have been the main fears of lawmakers in USA and UK.

Structure and Investment Policies of Institutional Investors

Whatever their type, the internal structure of institutional investors usually consists of sponsors or custodians, trustees and fund managers. The institution may be organized as a company (in which case there will be directors and not trustees) or a trust and its fund managers may belong to a separate asset management company. Day-to-day investment decisions are made by fund managers whose performance is judged on the basis of the returns they earn while trustees are accountable to investors or beneficiaries through sponsors. Trustees have a fiduciary duty to investors. An arms length relationship among these three constituents is maintained in the interest of professionalism and fairness. It is also provided usually that a majority of trustees and directors of asset management companies be independent of custodians of fund assets. In all institutional investors, accountability of fund managers to trustees is well established but that of trustees to beneficiaries, less so.

Investment strategies of fund managers are of three types.

- Active investing means making buying/selling decisions on the basis of fluctuations in the stock exchange price index. In order to diversify risk and remain liquid, a fund tries to go for a varied portfolio and avoids holding too many shares in one company. This has invited the charge that fund managers spread themselves too thin and in their desire to earn returns higher than those from stable portfolios, they shuffle them excessively and create turbulence in the stock market.

Table 7.2. *Restrictions on corporate ownership by institutional investors*

Type of institution	United Kingdom	United States of America	Japan	Germany
Mutual Funds	Cannot have large holdings in companies. Source: The Financial Services Act, 1986.	Tax penalties and regulatory restrictions if ownership exceeds 10% of a company's equity. Source: The Investment Company Act, IRS.	No restrictions.	No restrictions.
Banks	Bank of England may discourage ownership on prudential grounds. Capital adequacy rules discourage large holdings.	Shareholding banned or requires prior sanction of Federal Reserve Board. It must be passive. Source: The Glass-Steagall Act (abolished in 1999.)	Prior to 1987, could hold up to 10% of total shares in a company. Since 1987, the limit has been brought down to 5%. Source: The Anti-Monopoly Act	No restrictions apart some generous prudential rules.
Life Insurance Companies	—	Can hold up to 2% of total assets in a single company's securities and up to 20% in equities. Source: The New York Insurance Law	—	Can hold up to 20% of total assets in equities Source: The Insurance Law
Other insurance Companies	Self-imposet limits on fund assets to be invested in any one company stemming from fiduciary requirement of liquidity.	Control of non-insurance company prohibited. Source: The New York Insurance Law	Can hold up to 10% of company stock. Source: The Anti-Monopoly Act	No restrictions

(contd.)

(Table 7.2 contd.)

Type of institution	United Kingdom	United States of America	Japan	Germany
Pension Funds	Voluntary restrictions on assets to be invested in any one company as per fiduciary requirement of liquidity.	Must diversify. Source: The Employee Retirement Income Security Act, 1974. Public pension funds to follow indexation as investment policy and not to exercise voting rights. Source: The Federal Employees Retirement System Act, 1986.	—	—
General Provisions	Insider trading laws discourage large stakeholders from exerting control. Source: The Insider Dealing Act	For 5% stake in any company SEC must be notified. Antitrust laws prohibit vertical restraints. *Insider trading laws discourae active shareholding.* Creditor in control of a firm liable to subordination of its loans. Source: The Bankruptcy Case Law	—	Regulatory notification required for 25% ownership.

(Source: Stephen Prowse, Corporate Governance in an International Perspective, Bank for International Settlements, Economic Paper No. 41, July 1994)

- The second strategy is *indexing* where a fund chooses a particular price index, say Sensex or Nifty and then in a smaller way, it replicates the stock market by buying all the scrips included in the index. Thus good, bad, and indifferent – all types of shares find their way into its portfolio and changes in it exactly reflect the stock market changes.
  Both these strategies use the stock market price as the indicator of company performance and make their moves accordingly.
- The third strategy of relational or value investing means going behind the market price of shares and assessing the intrinsic worth of a company. This means assuming that intrinsic worth is different from current worth and to help realize the former, counseling is provided to management and a close relationship is built with it. Commitment, trust and long-term relations between the investor and investee companies are the hallmarks of this strategy. It represents dedicated capital and not transient capital of portfolio investment type.

So far as corporate governance is concerned, relational investing is the only strategy that can be thought of as an alternative to capital market monitoring. Of course, a big offloading by an institutional investor in the stock exchange is going to send shockwaves through the directors and executives of the concerned company but the essence of this action is to use capital market to discipline a company whereas relational investing tries to do so directly. Active investing uses stock prices for adjusting its portfolio and the work of constantly studying changes in the market, forecasting developments and making appropriate changes in one's portfolio is demanding. It leaves little time for governance of these companies. This is a paradox known as 'active investing, passive ownership.' Its reverse – 'passive investing, active ownership' denotes relational investing. As for indexation, at one level, it is said cynically that it is a very easy way of working and it leaves plenty of time for fund managers who then use it to monitor portfolio companies' affairs. However, at another level, competition among different institutional investors gives rise to free riding problem. A fund that wants to monitor a firm's performance will have to incur some costs which cannot be shared with other funds. The potential benefit of this action will however, be shared by other funds and so no fund manager will be willing on his own, to start such an action. Thus even here the scope for active monitoring is quite limited. Perhaps that is why the Federal Employees' Retirement Scheme Act in the USA provides that indexation will be the investment strategy of all public pension funds.

There exist two varieties of relational investing. In the older variety, a high standard of mutual respect between the investor and investee business can be observed. Investor's fund manager tries to be on close terms with the investee firm so as to understand the intricacies of its operations. He is given access because the firm knows that his objective is not simply to obtain inside information and trade on it in the market. The investor can also be active in governance issues because it does not want only to upstage the management but to help the business prosper. Warren Buffet's Berkshire Hathaway Fund is a good example of this type of relational investment.

In the new variety, institutional investors buy shares of a company in order to precipitate improvements in its performance. Such an investor is bent on a confrontation with incumbent management and it thereby hopes to get rid of inefficiency and lethargy. Lens, established by RAG Monks and Nell Minow and California Public Employees' Retirement System (CalPERS) are two well-known American institutions which practise this strategy.

Teachers Insurance and Annuity Association-College Retirement Equities Fund (TIAA-CREF), one of the largest pension funds in the USA is also active and both CalPERS and TIAA-CREF try to bring about improvement in the governance of investee companies. However, they are not as belligerent as Lens is and are highly selective in their activist role.

Generally most of the institutional investors tend to be portfolio investors, active in turning their portfolios around as per stock price fluctuations. They are not active in intervening in the affairs of investee companies. The older variety of relational investing is almost too good to be true.

Intervention by Institutional Investors

Takeover bids in the secondary capital market and institutional monitoring are seen as rival corporate governance mechanisms. This presupposes that they are independent of each other. However, the above analysis makes it clear that this is not so. Capital market is primary and institutional investors themselves depend on it while pursuing active investing and indexation strategies. Institutional monitoring in the 1990s resulted in the removal of takeover defenses which made takeovers easier. In other words, institutional investors have helped in strengthening corporate monitoring by secondary capital market. This is one more link between institutional investors and the capital market. Generally, institutional monitoring has limitations when there exists an active capital market. Relational investing flourishes in Germany and Japan precisely because there does not exist an active capital market there.

Another interesting observation is that institutional investors themselves have not evinced much interest in intervening in the affairs of portfolio/investee companies. In spite of a lot of discussion, there has been little *real* change after the Cadbury Committee's recommendations. Even when compelled by purely commercial consideration of protecting their investment, institutional investors have traditionally preferred informal, hush-hush discussions with incumbent managements. The time-honoured policy is to side with managements as far as possible. Institutional investors have always maintained that they do not have the time or the competence for intervention. They go to great lengths to avoid a public image of aggressiveness. They also find that news of any serious difference between institutional investors and an investee company gets instant media coverage, affects share price and reduces their elbow room for future action. It of course tips off rival institutions. There is no dearth of managers who fear that institutional investors may intervene excessively, in an inappropriate manner or under inappropriate circumstances because fund managers do not know that is required to be done.

Intervention invariably raises the issue of conflict of interest. Interests of lenders or creditors and shareholders are different. Creditors want regular interest payment and safety of the principal amount. Shareholders want dividends and appreciation of share price. When a company is not doing well, creditors' interest (getting interest and recovering principal) is opposite that of shareholders. Under adverse conditions, when the board recommends dividend payout, creditors may feel that it is a drain on company resources, impairing its ability to pay interest and return borrowed funds. Nominee directors of lending institutions might want to vote against dividend payout.

In India, the Industrial Development Bank of India (IDBI), the apex development finance provider to industry, reported that in 1998, it held equity in 600 companies out of 3000 companies to which it had lent money. Its investment objective in these 600 firms is different as compared to that of ordinary shareholders. It is supposed to be a friend, philosopher and guide, have long-term prospects before it and nurture firms and guide them through short-term problems. It is expected to wait patiently till teething troubles in the gestation period are over and ensure that firms become viable – thus more or less parenting the firms.

Many institutional investors have business relationships with portfolio companies and this makes them reluctant to interfere with management. For example, some institutional investors are subsidiaries of investment banks which are investment advisors to many companies. Insurance companies and pension funds have their corporate clients whose shares they may hold and so on. Sometimes directors of institutional investors and directors of portfolio companies share an understanding on issues concerning them as directors. Nominee or representative directors may be present in a board meeting which takes a particular decision and later, if it turns out to be detrimental to institutional investors they are put in an embarrassing situation. Nominee directors have to wear two hats in company meetings and they do not relish it.

Intervention by institutional investors in the 1990s has not resulted, uniformly, in higher returns to investee companies but has saddled them with some unenviable tasks. According to Monks, institutional investors are well-placed to raise issues of fairness such as criticism of excessive executive pay but their trustees do not have sufficient incentives to bring about sustained high returns in these companies. Trustees are subject to many political pressures which make them reluctant to interfere with management. This problem is acute in case of public pension funds in the USA. The government likes to use their funds to bridge budget deficits or to cover items which it cannot afford to disclose in the budget. Politicians' equations with large companies also come in the way of efficient monitoring by institutional investors. Therefore the question – who will guard the guardians becomes very important. In advocating institutional monitoring, are we not simply creating one more layer of control to take care of corporate accountability?

A frequent fear expressed is, that institutional investors might resort to insider dealing. They may use price-sensitive information gathered by them in the course of meetings and discussions with company managements, use it to their advantage in market operations and reduce the sanctity of market price. This is certainly a possibility and to counter it, fuller disclosures to shareholders and competition among institutional investors are essential. Legal provisions in the UK and the USA have been made mainly to prevent this from happening. Institutional investors must also maintain distance between market operations of asset management companies and their institutional representatives and adhere to the highest standards of professionalism.

Another charge leveled at institutional investors is that their awakening as shareholders has forced companies to resort to high dividend payouts and keep share prices high. In support of this point, it is argued that dividend payouts are consistently high in British and American companies as compared to German and Japanese ones. High payouts are supposed to harm surplus accumulation and organizational progress. On the other hand, they would also loosen the tight grip of management on organizational surplus and facilitate its transfer to shareholders. Assertion of shareholder value as the final goal of corporates is a major part of current corporate governance debate and so high dividends is not a problem but a necessary cure. Adherents of organizational perspective however, call this short-termism and they cry foul over this development.

Considering these pros and cons, Pozen's pragmatic cost-benefit approach to this contentious issue seems helpful. In sharp contrast to the Cadbury Committee, the OECD corporate governance principles support this position. OECD states that institutional investors should consider the costs and benefits of exercising their voting rights before making a move in this regard. Costs of intervention vary from a very high quantum of a proxy fight to a low one involved in informal consultations with investee company management. Benefits vary from increase in earnings, increase in share price to procedural reforms (which are difficult to relate to earnings but help set the house in order). Considering net benefits, the issues that institutional investors have found worth fighting for in the UK and the USA are linking executive pay to company's financial performance, opposing takeover defences, improvement in working of the Board of Directors through committee formation etc. (According to Pozen, separation between the positions of the board chairman and the CEO is not a worthwhile issue.)

Thus contribution of financial and institutional investors in corporate, monitoring is limited. Their initiatives in this respect take some specific forms.

Forms of Intervention

As mentioned above, institutional investors prefer informal, behind-the-scenes action. The scope for such action has today widened considerably thanks to associations of institutional investors. Stapledon has distinguished between:

Industry-wide and firm-level monitoring *and* direct and indirect monitoring.

Industry-wide monitoring includes actions such as lobbying with government, stock exchanges and regulatory bodies for suggesting changes in rules and regulations. Firm-level monitoring includes actions such as meetings with top managers of investee companies, discussions with non-executive directors, exercise of voting rights and even replacement of under-performing managers or directors.

Direct monitoring means that a concerned institutional investor itself carries out the task of oversight. Indirect monitoring means that the institutional investor acts through proxies – non-executive directors, institutional shareholders' committees or associations of institutional investors.

Actions of institutional investors in this regard can also be differentiated as routine and extraordinary actions. Routine action primarily means analysis of information about an investee company, in-house research and regular dialogue with company directors and top management. For regular meetings with the management, Charkham and Simpson recommend the following format:

a   a meeting after annual results are declared
b   one-to-one meeting with senior management
c   a site visit to factory
d   having at least one presentation from the company providing a full update on current trading and strategic thinking.

Extraordinary actions by institutional investors could mean any of the following:

- Sounding off company management regarding a specific concern.
- Attending or convening a shareholders' conference for discussing a specific concern.
- Approaching non-executive director or corporate advisor of an investee company either singly or along with other institutional investors.
- Joining coalitions of shareholders or institutional investors or leading them for bringing about changes in an investee company. The change usually means a change in the composition of Board of Directors or top management.
- Convening extraordinary general meeting and exercising voting rights in it, on resolutions calling for the removal of director/s or election of new director/s. Voting in annual general meeting may be treated as an extraordinary or routine matter depending upon the stand taken by an institutional investor in this regard.

- Putting a nominee director on the board of an investee company. (This practice is extensive in India but rare in other countries.)
- Litigation, initiated singly or with other institutional investors.

A Brief Review of Developments in the USA and the UK

USA

As shown in the appendix, mutual funds and investment trusts were prohibited from being active shareholders in 1940. After the Second World War, the US government offered substantial tax benefits to individuals and employers to provide for retirement income. Accordingly, plenty of funds were transferred from saving banks to pension funds. The Employment Retirement Income Security Act (ERISA), 1974 allowed private pension funds to invest in corporate securities to solve the problem of under-funding.

In 1986, the US government established the largest institutional investor in the world viz. the Federal Employees Retirement System. The Federal Employee Retirement System Act (FERSA), 1986, permitted federal employees to invest in equities. Other public pension funds – those for state and municipal employees – followed suit. This gave rise to fears of backdoor socialism. Nobody wanted a system in which government officers could pressurize corporate firms to act in a particular way by buying or selling their shares. So FERSA provided that indexation would be FERSA's investment strategy and its trustees, employees, members etc. would not exercise voting rights. In short, government employees' pension funds were brought to the capital market after ensuring that they could not, by virtue of their quantum, upset or dominate the market or incumbent managements.

The Council of Institutional Investors (CII) was formed in 1984 to bring institutional investors together. It actively lobbied Securities and Exchange Commission for liberalizing rules on shareholder action. It also developed policies on voting for its members. Department of Labour which regulates private pension funds, asked them to exercise their fiduciary duties under ERISA by participating in voting. In the early 1990s, the US investments in other countries increased sizably and pension funds which had invested in foreign companies were asked by the Department of Labour to vote their shares. Public pension funds remained outside the purview of this directive.

However, since the mid-1990s, public pension funds have also started becoming active, in spite of FERSA. Out of many public pension funds, only a few are involved in governance issues. CalPERS, TIAA-CREF have been mentioned above. The New York City Pension Fund is one more active fund. The touch of CalPERS was found to be electrifying and with its intervention, share prices and shareholders' wealth rose substantially.

UK

In this country, institutional investors have been very prominent and for a longer time as compared to other countries. Pension funds and insurance companies accounted for nearly half of the total corporate equities in 1994. Changes in the ownership pattern of equities can be seen from Table 7.3.

Table 7.3. *Percentage of distribution of equities in UK*

Owner	1963	1981	1994
1 Individuals	54.0	28.2	20.3
2 Overseas	7.0	3.6	16.3
3 Institutional investors			
a. insurance companies	10.0	20.5	21.9
b. pension funds	6.4	26.7	27.8
c. unit trusts	1.3	3.6	6.8
d. investment trusts	11.3	6.8	3.3
sub-total	**29.0**	**57.6**	**59.8**
4 Others	10.0	10.6	3.6
Total	100.0	100.0	100.0

(Source: Short, Keasey, 1997)

Institutional investors in the UK have now established their trade associations such as the National Association of Pension Funds (NAPF), the Association of British Insurers (ABI), the Association of Unit Trusts and Investment Funds (AUTIF), the Association of Investment Trust Companies (AITC) and the Institutional Fund Managers' Association (IFMA). Formation of these bodies has helped to solve the free-riding problem. These bodies have successfully fought against efforts to dilute shareholders' pre-emptive rights and to introduce non-voting shares. They have released statements on a number of issues such as buy-back of shares, pre-bid takeover defenses, disclosure of information in company reports, disclosure of non-audit relationship with auditors, executive remuneration and service contracts etc. These statements have been very influential. Many of their ideas have been incorporated in different committee reports, listing requirements, legislation etc.

In 1981, the Bank of England, the Stock Exchange, the Institutional Share-holders' Committee, the Confederation of British Industry and banks established the body — the Promotion of Non-Executive Directors (PRO NED). Their main objective was to strengthen the role of non-executive directors as a remedy to the problem of ineffectual boards that were unable to check the downslide in company performance. PRO NED also issued guidelines on the establishment of audit, remuneration committees and on the appointment process for non-executive directors. Its ideas were accepted by the Cadbury Committee. Sir Adrian Cadbury was the Chairman of PRO NED in 1985.

Institutional investors have been, time and again, asked to take a lead in developing a cadre of professional, independent directors to tone up corporate governance. PRO NED is the embodiment of this idea. It has been very effective. Apart from holding seminars and conferences to promote the role of non-executive directors, it has *helped* companies to find suitable directors. Around 1985, it was assisting in about 50 appointments a year. In fact, its work was a precursor to the Cadbury Code (1992). It now acts as a consultancy firm specializing in executive and director search.

The Pensions and Investment Research Consultants Ltd. (PIRC) was set up in 1986 by a consortium of public pension funds to advise them in respect of individual companies on a number of ethical and governance issues. Private pension funds and investment managers have also now become PIRC's clients. PIRC has enunciated a set of principles of corporate governance. It examines the compliance of individual companies with these principles, discusses its findings with a company and then publishes its views about the future line of action to be adopted by shareholders. Companies are also given a chance to hear and comment on these views before they are given to clients. PIRC simply advises. It is up to the client to decide how to vote. Still, companies prefer to modify their actions and plans rather than invite adverse comments from PIRC. PIRC's corporate governance principles include rather offbeat topics such as political donations by companies, environment policy etc. apart from the usual points.

The NAPF runs a Voting Issues Service covering more than top 350 companies. It provides:

a   A report on each forthcoming annual or extraordinary general meeting with details of proposed resolutions and its own opinion regarding which of them contains contentious issues.

b   A checklist showing how far a company met with various corporate best practices.

c   A three-month rolling calendar of forthcoming AGM dates and locations. The ABI has established a proxy-voting service which includes a report showing proposed resolutions of prominent companies that are likely to be contentious and action being taken on them by the ABI members.

CalPERS in Corporate Governance Movement

CalPERS is the acknowledged leader of institutional investors in corporate governance movement in the USA. It has been at the forefront of shareholder activism since the mid-1980s and through its various initiatives it has shown that institutional investors can add to shareholder value.

CalPERS is the largest public pension fund in the USA and the third largest in the world. State and local government employees as well as school district employees' in California constitute its membership. Total membership exceeds 10,50,000. A board of administration that has 13 members makes its investment policies. Active/retired employee groups elect 6 of the members, 2 are ex-officio government officers and 5 are appointed by the Governor/legislature. Being a public pension plan, CalPERS does not come under ERISA.

CalPERS' investment kitty consists of contributions made by both employees and employers and income from existing investments. Its investment portfolio is diverse and it consists of real estate, fixed income securities and equities. Securities are held in national and international entities. For domestic equity, it follows the indexation strategy. Its foreign holdings are partially indexed and are managed by outside managers.

CalPERS board members do not have an explicit fiduciary duty to monitor investment performance but it is considered to be a part and parcel of a prudent investor's job. This does not fit well with indexation strategy but CalPERS sticks to the belief that monitoring is necessary to enhance returns from an indexed portfolio.

In trying to improve the performance of portfolio companies, CalPERS' central belief has always been that shareholders must act like owners. It asserts that ownership of equity is a continuing process in which shareholders must discharge all the responsibilities that are entailed. So care and judgement must be continuously exercised.

In monitoring, CalPERS has generally concentrated on board performance in portfolio companies. It has looked at the performance of independent directors closely and has sought to make them effective. In 1995, its board approved a large funding commitment for relational investment in a few companies. This was a major shift in policy as it had previously held that it had neither the resources nor the expertise to run portfolio companies. Now it holds that it has to function as a catalyst for improved management and accountability. With this change, it is possible to discern two distinct phases in its efforts for corporate monitoring.

In the first phase i.e. roughly from 1985 to 1995, it mainly used shareholder proposals to bring about certain reforms such as elimination of poison pills as a takeover defense. In 1991, instead of filing proposals, it sought to meet independent directors of portfolio companies. Both these interventions have been used to focus on topics such as:

- excessive executive compensation
- shareholders' freedom to elect directors
- aligning interests of shareholders and managers
- directors' role in governance.

Towards mid-1990s, winds of change were sweeping across American boardrooms. The board of General Motors (GM) sacked its CEO and restructured management. The same thing was observed in other major corporations such as American Express, Chrysler, IBM, Kodak and Westinghouse. GM board went on to adopting a set of formal corporate governance guidelines and it took a cue from CalPERS' efforts in this regard.

In the first phase, it encouraged independent directors as a group to take more interest in governance. In the second phase, it is trying to get directors to account for their *individual* performance. It is also trying to influence directors to avoid multiple directorships, to increase their communication with managers etc.

In both these phases, CalPERS has focused on the following specific improvements:

- specification of more demanding qualifications for directorship
- proxy reform, particularly stressing the need for confidentiality in collection independence in tabulation and uniformity in treating abstentions and non-votes
- shareholder participation in selecting executive directors
- discontinuing staggered boards etc.

A number of studies have established that company performance has improved after CalPERS focused its attention on it. One study analyzed the effect of CalPERS initiatives in case of 42 companies between 1987 and 1994. It found that in the 5 years prior to its intervention, stock prices of these companies were below Standard & Poor 500 index by 66 %. In the 5 years period after the intervention they rose by 41% above the index. An update of the study in 1995 found that post-intervention stock performance of these companies had improved by 52.5%. Another study by the Gordon Group corroborated these findings and concluded that activism of shareholders led to a significant increase in shareholder value. This study also tried to judge the relative efficacy of different means of intervention and it concluded that shareholder proposals were a very cost-effective means of monitoring.

Situation in India

The Indian financial system was a bank-dominated one till 1991 and since then it has become a capital market-dominated system. In the earlier phase, public financial institutions and banks were originally expected to give direction and control the business economy. Massive loan assistance to business was given through public financial institutions and the programme was consolidated with nationalization of major commercial banks in 1969. Since these loans were advanced at concessional rates of interest, public financial institutions were asked to appoint nominee directors on the boards of borrowing companies and in case of very large loans, an option to convert a part of the loan into equity was also vested in them. However, these measures have been, by and large, ineffective. Private businesses made use of public money channelized through public financial institutions without accepting any accountability to them. In the UK and the USA appointment of nominee directors is considered, if at all, as a measure of the last resort. In India, the practice is 30-odd years old and now institutional investors are moving towards selectivity on this score.

The important question is: in our transition towards capital market domination, what role can we envisage for public financial institutions in monitoring corporate firms? They have massive non-performing assets and precarious financial health. Their lending policies are not governed by market forces and they continue to function in an irresponsible fashion.

They have lent money and made equity investments recklessly. They have encouraged unscrupulous companies to raise matching funds for projects through public issues. Their merchant banking divisions brought out many dubious issues during the primary market boom of 1995–96. They have recently raised money themselves through public issues at unjustifiable prices by window-dressing their accounts.

As D Basu (2003) avers, all this money has been frittered away because public financial institutions have destroyed shareholder value on a massive scale and they have helped private businesses to do the same. Instead of controlling private businesses, they degenerated into main instruments for primitive accumulation of capital.

In the foregoing analysis, several shortcomings of institutional investors operations have been mentioned. What has not been mentioned but is the biggest factor in India is, corruption. A nexus of politicians, business promoters, brokers and bank officers has destroyed capital that was painstakingly accumulated by small investors. In the 1990s, any promoter with some minimum scale of operations and political contacts could tap public financial institutions. Smaller, unknown promoters could use any of the accounting firms which work as fixers. Many public financial institutions have their favourite promoters who are always supported by them. Big borrowers and their agents usually ensure the appointment of their own candidates as chairman, managing director or directors of these bodies. These top office bearers ensure more loans to promoters that would be made to go bad. Public sector mutual funds have been used as common dumping ground for junk securities. This is how Indian Bank, Allahabad Bank, United Commercial Bank, Industrial Finance Corporation of India and Unit Trust of India have become bankrupt. They and other bodies continue to survive only because of massive government support which is nothing but an unjustifiable charge on public exchequer. This is the sorry state to which the lofty idea of development banking has been reduced in the 1990s. What is even more galling is the audacity with which businessmen continue to take pot-shots at these institutes for their bad governance. In the Indian Bank, the union of officers threatened to publish the names of top loan defaulters when it was incensed at a particularly vitriolic attack by a prominent businessman. The threat was enough to silence the critic.

In short, credentials of public financial institutions for participating in corporate monitoring are doubtful. Nor are they interested in the job as will be made clear in the UTI case below. Measures such as nominee directors and convertibility clause in loan agreements were thrust upon them in the past.

Still, they cannot be entirely excluded from corporate governance system. The system is too important to leave out possible contribution from any source, howsoever shaky. Even the provision for appointing nominee directors should be retained for selective, effective use in future.

The above may appear to be a harsh indictment of public financial institutions. However, from the case study of UTI – the oldest and the biggest mutual fund in the country – readers can judge for themselves that there is no exaggeration involved.

Unit Trust of India (UTI)

UTI was set up 1964 as a public sector mutual fund and pioneer institutional investor to assure steady, regular income to a large number of retail investors and to help develop the country's financial system. As a government-backed body, UTI attracted small investors in droves. By giving them regular, increasing dividend year after year and by coming out with innovative schemes to mop up savings, UTI won their trust and admiration. Till 1989, the UTI was a successful organization. There was no competition in the capital market then and small investors continued to pour their savings in the UTI kitty. (In 1988, public sector banks were allowed to set up mutual funds and private mutual funds also followed suit shortly.)

After 1995 however, its performance started slipping and soon it became a roller-coaster ride downhill. It faced a crisis in 1998 because of a large gap between the Net Asset Value (NAV) of units under its flagship scheme US-64 and their high repurchase price. The government bailed out UTI from this crisis and appointed the Deepak Parekh Committee to investigate and correct matters. The committee submitted a report but was unable to bring about any improvement in the working of UTI. In July 2001, there was another, bigger crisis which led to the arrest of UTI chairman — PS Subramanyan. The SS Tarapore Committee 2001 was appointed this time and it brought out, for the first time, details of the messy, murky state of affairs in UTI.

 Under the chairmanship of a former RBI deputy governor, UTI is now split up and its structure has been revamped.

As UTI began its operations in 1964, US-64 mobilized small savings on a very large scale and it came to occupy a central position in savings and investment schemes in the country. From a corpus of Rs. 5 crore, US-64 grew to Rs. 21,378 crore in 1998. This is impressive even after recalling that till 1988, it was the only mutual fund in the country.

After 1994, UTI's portfolio started taking a beating. On June 30,1998, NAV was Rs. 9.50 per unit. It became Rs. 5.81 in December 2001. In June 1998, repurchase price of units stood at Rs. 13.70. The difference represented a shortfall of Rs. 6605 crore in absolute terms. Thus value of units did not have any relationship to NAV or the underlying value of stocks. Even as value was getting eroded, higher dividends continued. These dividends were paid year after year without disclosing financial performance of any scheme. Between 1995 and 1997, dividend payment was made out of reserves but this fact was never brought out.

From an early date, UTI was saddled with a very large portfolio. As on November 30, 1998, there were 1426 companies in its portfolio. It had spread itself too thin. No professional skill was shown in picking up securities. So only 81 out of 1426 companies showed any capital appreciation. Investment in remaining 1345 companies had declined by approximately 45%. This decline was *not* related to general bearish conditions in the capital market.

On June 30, 1998, debt portfolio of US-64 was Rs. 7086 crore in which corporate debt amounted to Rs. 4200 crore. This amount was spread over 550 companies ostensibly to diversify and reduce risk. The top 10 companies accounted for Rs. 1700 crore or app. 40% of corporate debt and Rs. 2500 crore were spread over 540 companies. Among the top 10 borrowers were 5 public sector units whose borrowings worth Rs. 875 crore had turned non- recoverable.

In spite of such a large portfolio, growth sectors such as information technology and branded consumer goods were missed out. Poorly performing industries such as textiles had a large share of the portfolio. UTI had accumulated many illiquid and junk shares. Almost 95% of its portfolio was badly under-performing.

Though a mutual fund, UTI lent money like a bank. In 1986, the investment combination was 79:21 in debt and equity. In 1998 it had become 37:63. As investment in risk capital increased so heavily, the policy of distributing regular, increasing dividends should have been changed because it would have been unsustainable. That did not happen. So a false picture of superb performance was painted. Unfortunately it helped to hasten the inevitable downfall.

As combination investment changed, proportion of interest income in total income declined from 81% to 29%. To meet the annual dividend outgo, it became necessary to realize profit on equity investments. So good equities in pharmaceutical and FMCG sectors were sold at high prices and the trust was left with bad, illiquid securities.

Actually, lower debt in total investments does not have to mean lower cash inflow. Cash inflow declined because bad equities were selected. Investment and asset management decisions in UTI were not decentralized but were made at the highest level of management. Secondary market operations were carried out on the basis of consultation with some select brokers! With its own equity research cell, UTI should have done the job itself.

To ease the strain caused by a situation of uncertain revenue and regular cash outflow, UTI began to actively target corporate investors around 1995. This initially led to growth in assets but later it worsened the problems.

The UTI chairman and fund management team monitored day-to-day operations of the trust. At one point, there were 76 different schemes in operation but there were no separate teams of fund managers for different schemes. Inter-scheme transfers of funds were made without any independent view of the need of each scheme. There was no system of rewards and punishments for the fund management team. Nor was there any system of monitoring portfolio performance in a regular manner.

Till 1992, UTI functioned as an arm of the ministry of finance. It belonged to a cozy club of public sector banks, public financial institutions, the ministry and financial regulators. It had a rooster of friendly, uncritical journalists who could always manage to print adulatory features on UTI. If the secondary market needed support, the ministry called the UTI chairman who did the needful.

Because of this arrangement, UTI became a law unto itself and it never submitted to SEBI's regulations, SA Dave, ex-chairman, argued that UTI was a unique institution with its own structure of lending, underwriting and equity investment which had stood the test of time. It was also claimed that UTI had real estate and other assets such as unlisted debt which could not be valued on an on-going basis. Dave also claimed that UTI's disclosures were better than those of other mutual funds and that it had strong internal accountability. All these turned out to be hogwash.

Unprofessional management and lack of accountability led to corrupt deals with brokers and promoters in its investment decisions, particularly after 1994. It put money in defaulting companies such as Essar Oil, Malvika Steel, Usha Ispat, Prag Bosimi Synthetics, Punjab Wireless Systems, SIV Industries, SJK Steel Corporation, SVC Superchem etc. Amounts given away were substantial: Malvika Steel – Rs. 71 crore, Essar Oil – Rs. 56 crore, Usha Ispat – Rs. 12 crore. More investments were made in companies such as Elbee Services, Essar Steel, Ganesh Benzoplast etc. to hide past losses. Defaults in some investments did not lead to stoppage of loans to other companies in the same business group.

Under the chairmanship of PS Subramanyam, UTI invested in IPOs or new issues of dotcom companies, media and entertainment sector companies *against* the advice of its equity research cell. Companies such as Business India, Pritish Nandy Communications, Midday Multimedia and Zee Telefilms benefited and all these investments have now turned into bad debts. In 2001, money invested in non-convertible debentures of Himachal Futuristic Communications and Kopran Industries went straight to Ketan Parekh.

In 1999, UTI was suddenly seized with the issue of its responsibility in corporate oversight. It wrote to some blue chip companies such as Hindustan Lever Ltd., Nestle etc. and asked them to induct UTI nominees on their boards. Strangely enough, poorly performing companies were left out of this initiative. Companies that were approached, refused to comply and the move came to naught. It was initiated at the behest of the Deepak Parekh Committee which had stated that UTI could play a major role in moulding corporate governance to maximize shareholder value. In the past, UTI had never taken any stand on the governance of portfolio companies. It was content to toe the line either of government or of various promoters.

In short, lack of discipline, professional practices, regulation and accountability along with corrupt dealings led to havoc in UTI.

With such a poor record of management of own affairs, it follows that public financial institutions cannot be asked to force others to do so.

Appendix

Mutual Funds and Corporate Governance

Mutual funds have uncertain, heavy payouts which are mostly concentrated in the short run. Therefore they are not normally concerned with governance of portfolio companies. What is even more important is that legal rules in the USA and the UK prohibit them from being active owners of equity, except within specified limits. A brief look at the historical background of these rules is highly instructive.

In the USA in the 1930s, some mutual funds started taking a part in monitoring affairs of portfolio companies. They underwrote securities, participated in bankruptcy reorganizations and also management of portfolio companies. In 1935, 56 investment companies had controlling interest in 187 portfolio companies. The Securities and Exchange Commission (SEC) was not happy with this development. Its position was that a banker (or large portfolio investors) should not take part in the management and policy formulation work of industrial concerns. It did recognize that oversight by mutual funds and investment companies would resolve the organizational and informational problems of small, scattered shareholders and would bring expertise to the task of company oversight along with sufficient clout to get the required changes implemented. However, SEC felt that negative consequences of such a course of action would far outweigh the above benefits. These disadvantages would be:

1 investment of funds in a portfolio company only for protecting the already large investments made by an investment company
2 forcing an excessive dividend payout from a portfolio company
3 forcing a merger on terms disadvantageous to minority shareholders of a portfolio company
4 making an unwarranted change in the financial policy or capital structure of a portfolio company
5 failure of the investment company itself due to lack of diversification.

So SEC argued that directors and employees of mutual funds, investment companies etc. should not be allowed on the boards of portfolio companies. It succeeded in getting this view accepted in case of mutual funds. Even today, the portfolio of a mutual fund is divided into one regulated and another unregulated part. The former, accounting for 75% of total portfolio, is subject to a fragmentation rule which states that a mutual fund cannot advertise itself as diversified if it owns, in its regulated portfolio, more than 10% of the equity of any one company.

In India also mutual funds are normally not allowed to vote and participate in internal affairs of a company. Although it has been suggested that they should be allowed to vote in the interest of fairness to all shareholders (RH Patil, *Economic and Political Weekly*, November 2001), this is how matters stand.

8

Political Economy of Indian Corporate Governance

"Now comes this new fad of corporate governance. It is not enough for us to make profit; it must be made in a way that is acceptable to the West. So we are rushing once again into making fools of ourselves. Irrespective of the costs involved, everyone is talking of audit committees of the board and additional disclosures. Soon, issue of compliance certificates will become a racket. What will we gain out of it? You can either govern or be open. On top of a massive recession since 1997 which has taken away our profit, now comes this added cost. How unfair can you get?"

This is the reaction of a middle manager of a very large company, well-known for its progressive policies. In the same vein, there were these utterances of Rahul Kumar Bajaj (the chairman of Bajaj Auto and the ex-president of the Confederation of Indian Industry) at a seminar on corporate governance in 1996. He said it was common knowledge that managers and directors of Indian businesses engaged in questionable practices while being fully aware of what were ideal or desirable practices. Therefore no committee on corporate governance was necessary.

Both these views are cynical but fairly representative responses to a development which, in the perception of a large number of business people, is being thrust upon them by developed countries or foreign capital. This antagonistic reaction looks at corporate governance measures as a cost of globalization and not as a necessary reform for the development of capital market.

At the same time, two points in the views expressed above need to be acknowledged as valid. First, there is no sustained link between corporate governance measures and profits. Second, there is a danger of the substance of the matter getting lost in the mere form of committees and certificates. Indeed, *The Economist* had warned as early as in August 1997 that the corporate governance movement was focusing on very narrow rules and regulations with the result that producing rule books for the board had become something of a cottage industry.

What is noteworthy about the above reactions is first, their refusal to accept the necessity for structural reforms as suggested by the corporate governance movement and second, resistance to western ideas of governance allegedly because the Indian ground reality is different. A basic problem with such an approach is whether any economy today has the freedom to pursue its own path. Internationally mobile capital is giving impetus to a broad convergence in the world not only in corporate governance practices but many other social and cultural norms. Also, while the Indian situation certainly has many complex features and as stated in Chapter 5, is an amalgam of both the Anglo-American and the German-Japanese corporate governance systems, it is not unique. At the same time, correct understanding of this situation is essential before we try to change it in the light of the foregoing principles and guidelines.

Understanding Indian Reality

Bagchi (1999) has termed the Indian capitalism as Bungalow-Haveli-Chawl or BHC capitalism. The bungalow is the habitat of foreign capitalist and it symbolized British power in administration, finance and industry. The haveli is the habitat of Indian Shroff who also functions as trader, industrialist and stock-broker. The haveli symbolizes the power of Indian industrialists. The *chawl* is the habitat of workers and small entrepreneurs producing and marketing their ware on their own. It is a symbol of sweatshops subcontracting for big firms. These three types co-exist and have continuous interactions.

The business economy of India is thus very diverse. It covers small-scale traders and entrepreneurs, medium-size enterprises and large industrial houses. The enterprises carry out a whole gamut of trade, manufacturing and service activities. At the highest level, this economy is represented by three business associations – the Federation of Indian Chambers of Commerce and Industry (FICCI), the Associated Chambers of Commerce and Industry (ASSOCHAM) and the Confederation of Indian Industry (CII). CII is the youngest and the most dynamic business association today.

Foreign capital and foreign firms have existed in India for a very long time. Prior to independence, foreign firms dominated the economy. After independence, they were subject to severe curbs and the Foreign Exchange Regulation Act (FERA) restricted the power of foreign capital. Liberalization in the post-1991 period has meant the end/relaxation of most of these controls.

After independence, a large public sector, comprising giant companies producing infrastructural goods and services was created. Private sector companies were barred from large segments of consumer goods sector which were reserved for the small-scale industry. The latter has enjoyed a variety of incentives offered by the state, ranging from cheap finance to product and market reservations. Cheap finance through public financial institutions was available to large, private sector businesses also. Till 1980s, the state erected barriers to external entry and this consolidated the tendency for oligopolistic development. (Under British rule, the managing agency system had sown the seeds of this system.)

The modern Indian business class has developed under colonial rule against an apathetic British state. It has originated from traditional trading communities of the pre-colonial era. Till date, many Indian businesses are inclined towards quick, short-run profits sought by a trader. Their orientation is not that of a capitalist entrepreneur who continuously transforms the means of production in order to generate new opportunities for making profit. At the same time, this class has developed in opposition to imperialism and has been strongly nationalist. It is not a comprador class. (Nayar, 1998)

The dominant unit of capital in India is the business group or family. The giant corporation in the West was a single firm which diversified into related or linked areas. Its counterpart in India has been a business group or oligopoly, consisting of a number of legally independent firms, operating in unrelated areas but controlled by a single, central decision-making authority, usually a business family.

So far, these oligopolies have been highly stable due to their financial strength, market power and ability to pressurize the state to adopt measures for limiting the induction of foreign capital. Hazari and Dutt first drew attention to their stable nature. Stability does not mean peaceful sharing of the spoils. They compete with each other but in forms that are not easily identifiable. Instances of open or price-based competition have been few. Competition has been seen in forms such as rivalry in investment decisions and in creating production capacity, pre-emption of capacity, collaboration agreements etc. However, coming together through associations to influence state industrial policy and to win concessions for particular industries and also for the private sector as a whole has been a favourite strategy of Indian oligopolies. These associations have also been bases for collusion among competing producers. Collusion has meant suppression of price competition and joint manoeuvers against the state, organized labour and consumers.

Due to the primary role of the state in economic matters and protection from competition granted by it to businesses till recently, managing the regulators to avoid competition has been crucially important to Indian businesses. A strong nexus between businesses and politicians for creating and dividing monopoly rent existed in India till 1990s. Therefore Indian corporate governance been described as a cozy arrangement between politicians, bureaucrats and business groups (Vincent Cable, 1995). Under licence-permit raj, corruption became institutionalized in the economy. Steep rates of taxation in the late 1960s, gave rise to a tax evasion culture which quickly became all pervasive. (NR Narayana Murthy has mentioned the case of his friend whose house was being run as the guest house of his company so that all the household expenses could be shown as corporate expenses! [Rajiv Gandhi Institute of Contemporary Studies, Conference Papers, Section: Ethics and Governance in Private Sector, 52 p.])

Under the regime of high direct taxes in the 1960s, it was counter-productive to show high profits in the books. At the same time, new ventures had to be funded. So all businesses resorted to skimming the surplus in business. This was facilitated by means of parallel accounting systems. Skimming also helped to make payments to politicians, bureaucrats and other powerful interests in society. Initially banks were not allowed to advance loans against equity. So businessmen used to convert skimmed surplus or simply, business cash into deposits which were bankable assets. Banks used to accept such deposits as security against loans. These loans were recycled into fresh investments in business. Losers in this arrangement were minority shareholders who did not get a share in the new business. Alive to the reality of skimming at every level of business dealings, businessmen have always considered that daily involvement of a member of the controlling family is essential to ensure that employees and managers do not resort to skimming for personal expenditure. This has reinforced the hands-on management style of business family members.

Because of this background, Indian private sector reveals the following characteristics:

1 Inward-looking nature
2 Rent-seeking
3 Excessive diversification in order to have a finger in each pie. It is well known that in the 1960s, business groups used to procure licenses in every industry and take their own time to become operational.
4 Fragmentation of capacities as resources were not concentrated in core competencies. Small capacities got created in many fields.

Family controlled businesses reveal the following additional features:

- poor quality of products
- poor margins
- diffused business focus
- non-transparent operations and accounting practices
- owner's self-interest getting priority over company interest and
- no money to buyout competitors but no desire to sell out either. (They face shortage of money in spite of raising capital constantly either through institutional debt or public issue of securities.)

Although they have enormous clout, business oligopolies do not control the state and there have been shifts in their relative positions. Since the late 1970s, new oligopolies have emerged. State control was strict immediately after independence. Licensing policy was an important tool of exercising state control and licenses issued used to be shared among applicants to curb concentration of economic power. This started changing in the late 1970s. Licensing and control of capital goods gradually ceased to be allocative measures and instead became arbitrary instruments for attaining social goals. New business groups that emerged under these conditions found it easy to influence decisions, obtain licenses and clearances for technical collaborations and imports of capital goods. These new groups were not burdened with excessive diversification and less-than-minimum economic scale of operations which would result into a high unit cost of production. They also did not have outdated capital stock and so could go for latest technologies more easily. Therefore they took off swiftly and made spectacular advances. Reliance group of companies epitomizes this development. Thus between 1975–90, new oligopolies undermined old oligopolies and industrial capital was restructured.

An era of deregulation in financial markets has begun in the country since 1991 and a capital market-based financial system has been created. Foreign capital has entered the country in a big way and barriers to external entry have been almost withdrawn. Foreign institutional investors have been permitted to make portfolio investment in Indian companies. Indian businesses also have been given free access to foreign capital markets. Both old and new oligopolies have been forced to forge new strategies under the changed circumstances.

Response of Indian Business Houses

Indian companies were not prepared for competition from foreign companies for a number of reasons. These were:
- Smaller scale of operations leading to higher unit costs.
- Till the 1990s, cost of capital was kept high in order to boost the use of labour-intensive techniques. Interest rates were considerably lower in other countries during this period. So foreign companies had little capital constraint and they entered India with deep pockets to bear losses for a prolonged period.
- Labour legislation made downsizing very costly.
- Indirect tax structure was a source of comparative disadvantage.
- In some cases, the state actively supported foreign companies at the cost of Indian companies. For instance, counter guarantees were given only to Enron.

These factors and the actual behaviour of multi-national corporations (MNCs) have given rise to a fear of domination by foreign capital among Indian firms. The perceived inimical posture of the state has aggravated this feeling and strategies of MNCs have only served to reinforce it. Some foreign firms have bought off local firms and have replaced their well-known brands with own international ones. Other foreign firms initially took on local partners on an equal basis but later, having understood the Indian ground reality, they reduced them to a subordinate position or ousted them altogether. Some have used the ploy of announcing their intention of a vast expansion of capacity for which the Indian partner was unable to bring matching finance and was therefore discarded or put in a subordinate position. Another strategy has been to enter the Indian market in a joint venture with a local firm and also to set up, some time later, parallel 100% subsidiaries of their own. The subsidiaries are then nurtured with more resources and more modern technology while the joint venture lags behind and becomes useless or uncompetitive. Thus Indian firms have painfully realized that as compared to foreign firms, the only bargaining strength they have is local knowledge and contacts with government which cease to matter after the initial period.

Indian businesses have adopted a two-pronged strategy to meet the challenge of the liberalized regime. At one level, the strategy is political – articulation of its interests and pressurizing the state to accommodate them. At the other level, the strategy is entrepreneurial. It has involved restructuring of individual firms. Restructuring has meant downsizing, focusing on core competencies and consolidation, expansion and even diversification through mergers and acquisitions.

Articulation of Interest

Initially the business community was happy with the end of the regime of licence-permits but dismayed at the opening of the economy to foreign capital. Even in the initial euphoria over the reform package, business sector kept demanding curbs on imports in order to create a level playing field. The three business associations welcomed foreign direct investment but simultaneously demanded protection for local industry. FICCI's demand was that foreign direct investment should play a dominant role in infrastructure, leadership role in export sector and supportive role in all other sectors. Similarly it had demanded that takeover bids by MNCs should have the prior approval of government. Since 1997, a prolonged recession began in the economy and it prompted businesses to demand more active state role. In spite of the efforts to accommodate foreign capital, some observers feel that functioning of the bureaucracy has changed little since 1991 and the institutional arrangement remains in favour of large Indian companies which have established contacts with bureaucracy.

Business Restructuring

By international standards, there is excessive labour deployment in Indian enterprises and so, the first move of restructuring has meant shedding of labour or 'downsizing'. (Tatas diplomatically used the word 'rightsizing' to blunt the edge of this measure.) Labour legislation has until recently banned retrenchment and so firms have been forced to foot costly bills of the Voluntary Retirement Packages (VRS) for this purpose. Even public sector firms have carried out this measure and there have been some curious instances of public sector banks suddenly going into the red because of annual write-off portion of the VRS amount. Most of the firms have successfully completed this programme by overriding the weak resistance of trade unions and by resorting to arm-twisting and pressurizing wherever necessary. Simultaneously, changes are being made in labour legislation to facilitate easy exit.

The kind of restructuring that is necessary in the post-liberalization era has been carried out by MNCs such as Siemens, Asia Brown Bovery, Atlas Copco,

ITW Signode, Ingersoll-Rand etc. They have taken drastic measures such as shifting locations, pruning product ranges, reducing overheads and reducing debt to the minimum. Siemens has sold its telecom business and ABB – power. They have created export opportunities for their products. Some have started using their Indian operations as manufacturing/design base for other operations. Hindustan Lever Limited has increased its working capital turnover from 4.9 times in 1987 to 64 times in 1997 and asset turnover from 6 to 10 times during this period. It has not made a public issue to raise capital for a long time. Little or no debt, maximum use of working capital and reluctance to make capital investment – these are hallmarks of MNC turnaround strategy. They have also adopted new business models appropriate to changed market conditions.

Indian companies on the other hand, first raise capital and then think of ways to spend it. When it was easy to raise money in the capital market, many planned a big leap over their current operations which did not materialize (exception: Reliance). At the same time, the force of change was such that all the oligopolies have been forced to take a hard look at their over-diversified structures, to identify core competencies and to weed out outdated, inefficient parts. Thus Tatas have given up textiles and oil mills; Raymond has hived off its steel and cement businesses. Thapar group has withdrawn from the manufacture of nylon, edible oil, publishing and has begun to concentrate on paper and chemicals. Ranbaxy and Murugappa have professionalized their managements. Table 8.1 shows the changed focus of the bigger business houses in their activities.

All business groups have tried to set their house in order. Many instances of consolidation and divestment within business groups can be cited. The United Breweries (UB) group merged its seven breweries with UB Ltd. Distilleries in the group were merged with McDowell Ltd. Best and Crompton Engineering Ltd. in the group was sold to Polysindo group in Indonesia and other engineering companies were merged with UB Engg. Ltd. In Tata group, Tata Industrial Finance and Telco Dealers' Leasing and Finance Company were merged with Tata Finance. Ipitata Refractories was merged with Tata Refractories, a subsidiary of Tisco. A number of tea gardens were taken over by Tata Tea.

In the ITC group, the Welcom hotels of ITC Ltd. merged with the ITC Hotels Ltd. VST Industries Ltd. and ITC Ltd.'s tobacco division were merged. Similarly, in case of paper, Tribeni Tissues and ITC Bhadrachalam Paperboards Ltd. were merged with ITC's paper division. Within GP Goenka group, three chemical companies viz. Herdilla Chemicals, Herdilla Oxides & Electronics and Herdilla Polymers were merged.

The biggest amalgamation took place between Reliance Industries Ltd. and Reliance Petroleum Ltd. on 1st March 2002 for the purpose of consolidation. Apart from mergers within business groups, the pace of mergers and acquisitions among diverse businesses also quickened after 1997. Hindustan Lever Ltd. led the way with the acquisitions of Tata Oil Mills Ltd. and Brooke Bond Lipton

Table 8.1. *Changed focus in business houses*

No.	Group	Existing Areas	New/Proposed Areas
1	Tata	Steel, power, commercial vehicles, consumer electronics, cement, tea, coffee, paints, refrigerators and air-conditioners, financial services, information technology, computer software and projects, consultancy	Agro-technology, aviation telecom, software and consultancy
2	Reliance	Textiles, manmade fibres, plastics, petrochemicals	Oil exploration, oil refining, telecom, infrastructure, software, exports
3	BK-AV Birla	Cement, aluminium, fertilizers, iron, chemicals, textiles, engineering, tea, plywood	Oil refining, steel merchant banking, mutual funds
4	Mahindra & Mahindra	Automobiles, pharmaceuticals, chemicals, elevators, steel construction	Time share resorts, hotels financial services, real estate
5	ITC	Tobacco, cigarettes, paper, paper boards, hotels, financial and travel services	Biotechnology, breweries, investment banking, insurance
6	Ruia	Steel, power, textiles, shipping, port services	Oil refining, chemicals, leather, mutual funds

(Source: S Shiva Ramu, 1996)

India Ltd. (The latter had itself taken over a number of companies such as Kissan, Milkfood Ice-cream, Kothari General Foods, Quality, Dollops Ice Cream etc. earlier.)

While the writing on the wall is clear to every business, most of them have not been able to restructure themselves successfully. Some old, entrepreneurial families have declined while others have been better off. Among the old conglomerates, Tata, Birla, Singhania, Goenka, Thapar, Ruia, Kirloskar groups have retained their positions as large conglomerates. Yet the list of major investment projects undertaken in the 1990s is dominated by new groups such as Reliance, Hinduja, Mittal etc. Reasons for decline of businesses have been varied. For instance, lack of professionalism has cost Scindias, dear. Intra-clan disputes have harmed Shri Ram and Birla groups. Sarabhai group has declined because of excessive centralization of authority while poor financial management has harmed Modi group.

Since software sector experienced the highest growth in the 1990s, restructuring plans of many businesses meant joining this sector. Mahindra & Mahindra, Larsen

& Toubro, BSES, Siemens, Blue Star and Birlas already had their software businesses which they now wanted to concentrate on. Kalyani and Munjal groups talked of IT-enabled services. The stock market's initial perception of the software sector was so favourable that with the announcement of mere entry into it, share prices of the above businesses zoomed up. That phase of euphoria is now over as it is realized that this sector too, is subject to cyclical growth.

In a bid to embrace new business models, many textile mills got into entertainment business and created swanky shopping malls. Lakme changed into a retail chain. Nicholas Piramal tried to grow through joint ventures. Domestic pharmaceutical companies such as Lupin Laboratories, Wockhardt, Sun Pharma put together their own research teams in a bid to imitate the success of Ranbaxy and Dr Reddy's Laboratories. Many business groups also brought in reputed management consultants – particularly McKinsey who advised them to get focused.

Cutting down workforce, selling property and closing down loss-making divisions/businesses constituted the first phase of restructuring. Most businesses stopped there. Only a few showed deeper commitment and willingness to go for radical ideas. Even they have failed to convert their initiative into sustained, better financial performance. Basu (2003) takes a hard look at these businesses and concludes that all of them have *lost* rather than created shareholder value. He is particularly scathing in his criticism of KM Birla, Tata, Murugappa, Raymond, Godrej and Nicholas Piramal groups. As compared to MNCs, Indian businesses have been loath to consider the hard options. Therefore even when they have talked of being focused, they have actually become more diversified (KM Birla group). The stark fact is that Indian companies have still not developed a model of growth in a globalized business environment.

Changes in Capital Market

Given the global mobility of capital, no capital market can remain static today. There have been some positive developments in it after the shakeout process from 1992–98. The stock market now stands polarized between performing and non-performing companies. Foreign institutional investors entered the market in 1992 but they lost a lot of money till 2000. Now however, they and private mutual funds are bringing judgement and discrimination to their operations. This is reflected in better choice of companies by them and also in the speed with which they move out of companies as signs of trouble appear. Under the weight of their actions many positive changes can be seen in the capital market. These changes are summarized in Table 8.2.

Coming Back to Corporate Governance in India

Tussle between foreign and Indian capital since globalization began in 1991 constitutes the backdrop of discussions on corporate governance in India. The

Table 8.2. *Changes in capital market after liberalization*

Feature	Before 1992	After 2000
Corporate objective	Asset growth and size, diversification and big projects	Low capital growth
Preferred activity	Raise capital as loans from banks or equity from public/mutual funds	Capital turnover and yield, growth in profitablity, shareholder value
Preferred industries	Capital intensive ones such as steel, petro chemicals, refinery, power	Any industry which offers prospects of growth
Investment horizon	Long-term	Short-term
Investor expectation	Dividend plus bonus	Capital appreciation, shareholder value
Investment tool	Impressions, no serious research	Inside information, research, judgement
Company practices	Anti-investor	Leaning towards investors. More disclosure. Important companies hold analysts' meetings twice a year
Public financial institutions	Inspired trust as they were state-owned. Their support was considered a point in favour of any project.	As lacunae in their working are reveled, public trust has evaporated.
UTI	Dominant player in equities. The only player till 1988.	Multiple players. Foreign intitutional investors and private mutual funds are more professional.
Stock marke	Rife with insider trading and price rigging. Brokers manipulated tips to push stock prices up or down.	Incidence of price rigging reduced.
Regulation	Little by Controller of Capital Issues. Mutual funds were lords were lords unto themselves. Brokers and companies flouted stock exchange rules.	SEBI's regulations are becoming extensive and effective. Rules have been made for mutual funds, depositories, portfolio management, against insider trading etc.

(Source: D Basu, 2003)

foreword to the Confederation of Indian Industry code of desirable corporate governance practices stated that this topic became very important at the juncture of integration of Indian economy with global economy and at the time when the Indian industry began striving for international competitiveness.

It has been opined that the immediate motive behind the initiation of the corporate governance debate in the country was the need to give an assurance to foreign creditors that their claims would not get the short shrift accorded to Indian creditors. It is well-known that financial institutions have been treated shabbily by their corporate borrowers in India and that the former therefore have huge non-performing assets. There is a general feeling that far greater importance has been given to foreign capital. The reason is not far to seek – unlike the captive capital of indigenous public financial institutions, this capital is highly mobile and will be withdrawn if some basic governance rules are not observed. In this connection, Murthy (1998) has raised one important question: can adequate support of new stakeholders be ensured while problems of old stakeholders remain unattended? The grievances of old stakeholders of Indian companies:

- cheating of investors and depositors
- default in payment
- evasion of excise duty
- nexus of corruption between managers and politicians
- insider trading and cornering of shares
- disregarding rights of minority and institutional shareholders.

The requirements of global capital will be clear from the following tables. It can be clearly seen that both corporate level and institutional or structural factors are considered here.

Table 8.3. *Importance of corporate level factors when selecting emerging market companies*

Sl. No.	Most Important Corporate Level Factors	Weight
1	distinction between company and family interests	4.5
2	clearly defined governance arrangements	4.4
3	accuracy of financial reporting	4.4
4	enforceable minority shareholder protection	4.3
5	use of performance-based compensation	4.3
6	timeliness of financial reporting	3.9
7	coverage of financial reporting	3.9
8	presence of non-executive directors	3.9
9	establishment of conflicts of interest committee	3.3

Table 8.4. *Importance of institutional factors when selecting emerging market countries*

Sl. No.	Most Important Institutional Factors	Weight
1	enforceablity of legal rights and contracts	4.5
2	quality of economic management	4.3
3	independence of judiciary/quality of legal system	4.0
4	level of corruption	3.9
5	predictability and level of taxation system	3.9
6	quality of accounting standards	3.8
7	effectiveness of regulatory system	3.8
8	administrative efficiency of government	3.5
9	effectiveness of banking sector	3.3
10	scale and liquidity of local investment market	3.3

(Factors have been ranked from 5 to 1, with 5 showing highly relevant and 1 irrelevant factor.)
(Source: McKinsey, Emerging Market Investor Opinion Survey, 2001)

The following differences between developed countries and developing or 'emerging' countries as regards corporate governance should be noted at this juncture:

Developed countries	Developing countries
Agency problem is the central corporate governance problem	Expropriation problem i.e. conflict between majority shareholders and managers on the one hand, and outside shareholders, other stakeholders on the other, is the central corporate governance problem.
Corporate governance movement saw voluntary corporate-level response first. It was sufficiently large. Following scams, legal and regulatory changes were made subsequently.	Very little voluntary corporate-level response was seen. After changes were made in the legal, regulatory set-up, compliance is now taking place.
Legal, regulatory framework surrounding corporate action is fairly efficient.	Legal regulatory framework, though impressive on paper, is weak in enforcement.

Thus agency costs and exuberance of executives have not been Indian concerns in corporate governance reforms. This is because business family members may not have been the best managers but they have always taken their responsibilities seriously and have been willing to apply themselves diligently. Due to the presence of powerful owner-managers and absence of self-perpetuating management by professionals as seen in the west, Indian priorities in corporate governance have been different.

Corporate governance reforms in developed countries have revolved around best practices codes, a fashion started by the Cadbury Committee and revolving today around the OECD principles. Given the structural differences between them and emerging countries, these codes and principles mean one thing in developed countries and something very dilute and weak in the latter.

Nonetheless, a lot of discussion of the Cadbury Committee report took place in 1996–97 in newspapers in India. Three authoritative committee reports suggesting improvements in the Indian corporate governance structure are available till date:

1   The Confederation of Indian Industry, Code of Desirable Corporate Governance – (1997)
2   The Kumar Mangalam Birla Committee (appointed by SEBI) Report – (2000)
3   The RH Patil Advisory Committee (appointed by RBI) Report – (RBI, 2001)

Out of these, the Birla Committee report has had the maximum impact on corporate practices in the country. Its recommendations have been covered in Chapter 6, *Appendix*. They have brought about a substantially improved quality of disclosures by listed companies.

In the opinion of the Patil Committee, listing agreement is a weak instrument to bring about the necessary changes in this regard. The reasons are:

1   Penal provisions for non-compliance are not strong enough in case of the listing agreement. Stock exchanges cannot even delist non-complying companies. Penal action is likely to hurt investing community more than the management of the defaulting company.
2   The number of non-listed companies is not insignificant. As per a report in *Businessworld* (19 November 2001) investment, income and gross fixed assets of all the unlisted companies were 32%, 25% and 16% respectively of those of all listed companies in the year 2000. These unlisted companies remain outside the scope of these regulations and indeed, they are one reason why companies prefer not to list their shares.
3   Many companies list their securities on regional stock exchanges which have little organizational resources for monitoring and for ensuring compliance.

Therefore the Patil Committee has recommended that provisions in Clause 49 (of listing agreement) be incorporated in the Companies Act and additional penal provisions be made for their violation. It has recommended that the work connected with listing of securities and the enforcement of penal provisions for any major violations of listing rules be entrusted to a designated central authority. (Central Listing Authority has been set up on 10 April 2003 by SEBI.) It also wants a clear definition of the Board of Director's duties in the light of the OECD principles to be incorporated in the Companies Act.

Its other recommendations are:

● Company promoters to fully disclose their direct, indirect and total holdings and any change in their controlling stake by 1% and more.

- Disclosure in the annual report of all payments received by auditors over and above their fees.
- Minimum strength of directors of companies with net worth of Rs. 15 crore and above to be 10 of whom 5 to be independent directors. (These independent directors will not include nominee directors.)

As regards insider trading, the committee has stated pragmatically that frequent, timely and exhaustive disclosure of all price sensitive information to shareholders is the only way to control its incidence.

Contributions of these committees are very important. They have begun to bridge the gap between lofty rules and regulations on the one hand and deceitful practices on the other. In the transition to capital market-based financial system being seen in the country, secondary capital market and more stringent but selective control by SEBI, within the framework of up-to-date company law will have to ensure improvement in the quality of corporate governance in the long run.

Better protection of investors and more effective implementation of existing legal and other provisions will be very important. In the mean time, the following measures will also have to pitch in:

- Better oversight by company boards.
- Better contribution by institutional investors. Withdrawal of state protection and pursuit of more commercial policies by public financial institutions will lead to better financial discipline among borrowing businesses. Investment by foreign institutional investors and foreign listings of securities by Indian businesses will lead to greater transparency.

Finally, greater product market competition and reduced state protection will bring down the incidence of rent-seeking in Indian businesses. Under the imperatives of global capital flows, changes outlined above will have to take place in India.

In the absence of developed markets and effective governance arrangement, managements can easily steal from shareholders and majority shareholders can steal from both minority shareholders and the public. Also corporate misconduct and mal-performance can remain undetected for a long time. If this is to be prevented and the capital market-the most important indicator of economic progress – is to be developed, corporate governance reforms are absolutely essential.

In the first chapter, a distinction was made between narrow and broad definitions of corporate governance. The former generally mean improved board practices in the interest of greater managerial accountability. However, it is necessary to shift emphasis from Board of Directors to disclosure and communication. In the broad view regarding corporate governance, individual firms do not matter much, the capital market does. Better disclosures enable the capital market to function more efficiently. Policy implications of our entire analysis boil down to: better disclosure by firms and efforts to enhance capital market efficiency by the regulators.

Bibliography

Ahluwalia, Isher Judge, IMD Little (eds.): *India's Economic Reforms and Development, Essays for Manmohan Singh*, Oxford University Press, New Delhi, 1998.

Aoki, Masahike, Managerialism Revisited in the Light of Bargaining – Game Theory, *International Journal of Industrial Organisation*, Vol. 1, 1983, 1–21.

Aoki, Masahike, Hyung-Ki Kim (eds.): *Corporate Governance in Transitional Economies: Insider Control and The Role of Banks*, IBRD, Washington D.C., 1994.

Ararat, Melsa, Mehmet Ugur: 'Corporate Governance in Turkey: An Overview and Some Policy Recommendations', *Corporate Governance: The International Journal of Business in Society*, Vol. 3, No. 1, 2003.

Backman, Michael, (Revised Ed.): *Asian Eclipse, Exposing the Dark Side of Business in Asia*, John Wiley & Sons (Asia) Pvt. Ltd. Singapore, 2001.

Bagchi, Amiya Kumar (ed.): *Economy and Organization, Indian Institutions under the Neoliberal Regime*, Sage Publications, New Delhi, 1999.

Bain, Neville, David Band: *Winning Ways Through Corporate Governance*, Macmillan Press, London, 1996.

Balasubramanian, N (ed.): *Corporate Boards and Governance,* Sterling Publishers, New Delhi, 1998.

Basu, Debashis: *Face Value, Creation and Destruction of Shareholder Value in India*, Kensource Business Books, Mumbai, 2003.

Baum, DJ, NB Stiles: *The Silent Partners: Institutional Investors and Corporate Control,* Syracuse University Press, Syracuse, NY, 1965.

Baums, Theodor, Philipp W. Randow: *Shareholder Voting and Corporate Governance: The German Experience and the New Approach*, International Bank for Reconstruction and Development, Washington D.C., 1994.

Bavly, Dan A: *Corporate Governance and Accountability: What Role for the Regulator, Director and Auditor?*, Quorum Books, 1999.

Berle, Adolf, Gardiner, Means, *The Modern Corporation and Private Property*, Macmillan, New York, 1932.

Bhide, Amar: Efficient Markets, Deficient Governance, *Harvard Business Review*, November–December, 1994.

Blair, Margaret M: *Ownership and Control: Rethinking Corporate Governance for the Twenty First Century*, The Brookings Institution, Washington DC, 1995.

Bowen, William G: *Inside the Board Room*, John Wiley & Sons Inc., New York, 1994.

The Best Boards, *Business Today*, May 7–21, 1997, 62–83.

Burnham James: *The Managerial Revolution*, John Day Company, New York, 1941.

Cable, Vincent: 'Indian Liberalisation and the Private Sector in Cassen', Joshi (eds.): *India, the Future of Economic Reforms*, 1995, op.cit.

Cadbury, Adrian: *Report of the Committee on the Financial Aspects of the Corporate Governance*, December, 1992. Gee & Co. Ltd., London, 1992.

Business India, December 2–15, 1996.

Carroll, Glen R, David J Teece (eds.): *Firms, Markets and Hierarchies – The Transaction Cost Economics Perspective*, Oxford University Press, Oxford, 1999.

Cassen, Robert, Vijay Joshi (eds.): *India, the Future of Economic Reforms*, Oxford University Press, New Delhi, 1995.

Chalam, GS Iyer, VH Mulwad, UR Deshmukh: *Corporate Governance Practice in India and Internationally*, Everest Publishers, Mumbai 2000.

Chandrasekhar, CP: Firms, Markets and the State: An Analysis of Indian Oligopoly in AK Bagchi (ed.) *Economy and Organization, Indian Institutions under the Neoliberal Regime*, Revised Ed. 2001, op. cit.

Charkham, Jonathan, Anne Simpson: *Fair Shares, the Future of Shareholder Power and Responsibility*, Oxford University Press, Oxford, 1999.

Chew, Donald H (ed.): *Studies in International Corporate Finance and Governance System: A Comparison of the US, Japan and Europe*, Oxford University Press, New York, 1997.

Charkham, Jonathan, Anne Simpson: *Fair Shares: The Future of Shareholder Power and Responsibility*, Oxford University Press, Oxford, 1999.

Clarke, Thomas, Elaine Monkhouse (eds.): *Rethinking the Company*, Pitman Publishing, London, 1994.

Conger, Jay, David Sinegold, EE Lawler III: Appraising Board Room Performance, *Harvard Business Review*, January–February, 1998.

Cosh, AD, A Hughes: The Anatomy of Corporate Control: Directors, Shareholders and Executive Remuneration in Giant US and UK Corporations, *Cambridge Journal of Economics*, 11, 1987, 285–313.

Colvin, Geoffrey: Bad Boards Bad Boards, Whatcha Gona Do? *Fortune 500* Vol. 139, No. 8, April 1999.

Crum, Roy L, Itzhak Goldberg: *Restructuring and Managing the Enterprize in Transition*, IBRD, EDI Learning Resources Series, 1998.

Cyert R.M. and J.G. March: *A Behavioural Theory of the Firm*, Prentice-Hall, Englewood Cliff, N.J., 1963.

Dahl, R.A., Power to the Workers?, *New York Review of Books*, November 19, 1970, 20–24.

Davis, E Philip, Benn Steil: *Institutional Investors*, The MIT Press, Cambridge, Massachusetts, 2001.

Dayton, Kenneth N: Corporate Governance: The Other Side of the Coin, *Harvard Business Review*, January – February, 1984.

De Angelo Harry, Linda De Angelo: "Proxy Contests" *The New Palgrave Dictionary of Money and Finance*, Machmillan Press Ltd, London, 1992.

Degnbol-Martinussen, John: *Policies, Institutions and Industrial Development,*

158   *Corporate Governance and Indian Scenario: An Introduction*

Coping with Liberalization and International Competition in India, Sage Publications, New Delhi, 2001.

Demsetz, H: 'The Theory of the Firm Revisited', *Journal of Law, Economics and Organization*, Vol. 4, No. 1, Spring 1988, 142–61.

Demsetz, HK Lehn: The Structure of Corporate Ownership, Causes and Consequences, *Journal of Political Economy*, Vol. 93, No. 6, December, 1985, 1155–77.

D'Souza, Errol: Structure of Corporate Finance and Corporate Governance in India, *Economic and Political Weekly*, Vol. XXXV, No. 48, November 25, 2000.

Dunlavy, Colleen A: Corporate Governance, in Late Ninteenth Century Europe and the US – the Case of Shareholder Voting Rights, in Hopt, Kanda, Roe, Wymeersch and Prigge: *Comparative Corporate Governance: the State of the Art and Emerging Research*, Clarendon Press, Oxford, 1998 op.cit.

Dutta, Sudipt: *Family Business in India*, Response Books, New Delhi, 1997.

Fama, E.F., Jensen, M.C.: Agency Problems and Residual Claims, *Journal of Law and Economics* Vol. 26, June 1983, 301–26.

General Motors Board of Directors, GM Board Guidelines on Significant Corporate Governance Issues, Detroit, March, 1994.

Ghosh, DN: Corporate Governance and Boardroom Politics, *Economic and Political Weekly*, Vol. XXXV, No. 46, November 11, 2000, 4010–14.

Godbole, Madhav: Corporate Governance: Myth and Reality, *Economic and Poltical Weekly*, Vol. XXXVII, No. 30, July 27, 2002, 3094–3102.

Gordon, Lilli A., John Pound: *Governance Matters: An Empirical Study of the Relationship Between Corporate Governance and Corporate Performance*, The Corporate Voting Research Project, John F Kennedy School of Government, Harvard University, June 1991.

Goswami, Omkar: *Corporate Bankruptcy in India, A Comparative Perspective*, Development Centre Studies, OECD, 1996.

Goswami, Omkar, Rakesh Mohan: Industry: An Unfinished Agenda in Kelkar, Vijay L., VV Bhanoji Rao (eds.): *India, Development Policy Imperatives*, Tata McGraw- Hill Publishing Co. Ltd., New Delhi, 1996.

Gower, ECB: *Principles of Modern Company Law*, Stevens & Sons, London, 1969.

Grossman, SOD Hart: Takeover Bids, the Free-Rider Problem and the Theory of the Corporation, *Bell Journal of Economics*, 11, 1980, 42–64.

Group of Thirty: *The Evolving Corporation: Global Imperatives and National Responses*, Washington DC, 1999.

Gupta, LC: Excellence of the Board of Directors, *Vikalpa*, Vol. 11, No. 4, 1986.

Gupta, LC, Archana Sekhar: *Controlling Corporate Sickness, Lessons and Experiences for Managers and Bankers*, Oxford University Press, Bombay, 1988.

Gupta, LC: *Corporate Boards and Nominee Directors*, Oxford University Press, New Delhi, 1989.

——— *Indian Shareowners, A Survey*, Society for Capital Market Research and

Development, New Delhi, 1991.

———— What Ails the Indian Capital Market? *Economic and Political Weekly*, Vol. 33 No. 29–30 July 18, 1988, 1961–96.

Hannah, Leslie: *The Rise of the Corporate Economy*, Methuen, London, 1976.

Hanson, James A., Sanjay Kathuria (eds.): *India: A Financial Sector for the Twenty-First Century*, Oxford University Press, New Delhi, 1999.

Harper, John: *Chairing the Board, A Practical Guide to Activities and Responsibilities*, Kogan Page Ltd., London, 2000.

Hart, Oliver: Corporate Governance: Some Theory and Implications, *Economic Journal*, 185 (438), May 1995.

Hazari, RK: *The Structure of the Corporate Private Sector: A Study of Concentration, Ownership and Control*, Asia Publishing House, 1966.

Hermalin, BM, Weisback: The Determinants of Board Composition, *Rand Journal of Economics*, Vol. 19, 1998, 589–606.

Hellwig, Martin: On the Economics and Politics of Corporate Finance and Corporate Control in Xavier Vives, (ed.) *Governance, Theoretical and Empirical Perspectives* Cambridge University Press, UK, 2000.

Herman, ES: *Corporate Control, Corporate Power*, Cambridge University Press, Cambridge, 1981.

Hopt, KJ, H Kanda, MJ Roe, E Wymeersch, S Prigge: *Comparative Corporate Governance: the State of the Art and Emerging Research*, Clarendon Press, Oxford, 1998.

IDBI (Industrial Development Bank of India), *IDBI Guidelines for the use of Nominee Directors*, Bombay, January, 1986.

Ide, Masasuke: *Japanese Corporate Finance and International Competition, Japanese Capitalism versus American Capitalism*, Macmillan Press Ltd., London, 1998.

Jensen, Michael C: Agency Costs of Free Cash Flow, Corporate Finance and Takeovers, *American Economic Review*, Papers and Proceedings, 76, 323, 1986.

———— *A Theory of the Firm, Governance, Residual Claims and Organizational Forms*, Harvard University Press, Massachusetts, 2000.

Jensen, MC, WH Meckling: Theory of the Firm, Managerial Behaviour Agency Costs and Ownership Structure, *Journal of Financial Economics*, Vol. 3, No. 4, 1976, 305-60.

Jenson, M, Kevin Murphy: Performance Pay and Top Management Incentives, *Journal of Political Economy*, Vol. 98, 1990, 225–63.

John, Sujit: Code to Clean Up Corporate Conduct, *Times of India*, May 7, 1997.

Joseph, Mathew, Rupa Nitsure, Madan Sabnavis: Financing of Indian Firms: Meeting the Needs and Challenges of the Twenty-First Century in Hanson, Kathuria (eds.): *India: A Financial Sector for the Twenty-First Century*, 1999, op.cit.

Joshi, Vasudha: *Evolution of Better Practices: The Case of Indian Boards*, Chartered Secretary, Vol. 33, No. 3, March 2003.

Chartered Secretary, Vol. 33, No. 3, March 2003.

——— Institutional Investors and Corporate Governance, *Management Accountant*. Vol. 37, No. 11, November 2002.

——— Voting Rights and Corporate Governance, *Chartered Secretary*, Vol. 31, No. 1, January 2001.

Joshi, Vijay, IMD Little: *India's Economic Reforms, 1991–2001*, Oxford University Press, New Delhi, 1996.

Karpoff, Jonathan M, M Wayne Marr Jr, Morris G Danielson: *Corporate Governance and Firm Performance*, Blackwell Publishers Ltd., Oxford, 2000.

Kathuria, Vinish, Shridhar Dash: Board Size and Corporate Financial Performance: An Investigation, *Vikalpa*, Vol. 24, No. 3 July–September, 1999.

Keasey, Kevin, Steve Thomson, Mike Wright (eds.): *Corporate Governance, Vol. I to IV*, Edward Elgar Publishing Ltd., The International Library of Critical Writings in Economics, UK, 1999.

——— *Corporate Governance, Economic Management and Financial Issues*, Oxford University Press, UK, 1997.

Kennedy, Allan: *The End of Shareholder Value*, Orion Business Books, London, 2000.

Kini, O, W Kracaw, S Mian: Corporate Takeovers, Firm Performance and Board Composition, *Journal of Corporate Finance*, 1, 1995, 383–412.

Kose, John, Lemma W. Senbet: Corporate Governance and Board Effectiveness, *Journal of Banking and Finance*, Vol. 22, 1998.

Kumar Mangalam Birla Committee on Corporate Governance, Report, SEBI, Mumbai, 2000.

La Porta, Rafael, Florencio Lopez-de-Silanes, Andrei Shleifer: Corporate Ownership Around the World, *Journal of Finance*, 54 (2), 1999, 471–517.

Lauenstein, Milton C: Preserving the Importance of the Board, *Harvard Business Review*, July–August, 1977.

Lazonick, William, Mary O' Sullivan: *Big Business and Corporate Control in International Encyclopedia of Business and Management*, (ed.) Malcolm Warner, Vol. 1, 365–85, Routledge, London, 1996.

Lehmann, Jean-Pierce: Corporate Governance in East Asia and Western Europe: Competition, Confrontation and Co-operation in Oman, Brooks, Foy (eds.): *Investing in Asia*, Development Centre, OECD, Paris, 1997, op.cit.

Lorsch, Jay, Samantha K Graff: *Corporate Governance*, International Encyclopaedia of Business and Management, Malcolm Warner, (ed.), 1996, op.cit.

Mace, M: *Directors: Myth and Reality*, Harvard Business School Press, Boston, MA, 1971.

——— The President and the Board of Directors, *Harvard Business Review*, March–April 1972, 37–49.

Marshall, Alfred: *Industry and Trade*, Macmillan, London, 1920.

Manne, Henry G: Mergers and the Market for Corporate Control, *Journal of Political Economy*, Vol. 73, 1965, 110–210.

Marris, Robin: *Theory of Managerial Capitalism*, Macmillan, London, 1964.

Marris, Robin, Adrian Wood (eds.): *The Corporate Economy: Growth, Competition and Innovative Potential*, Macmillan & Co. Ltd., London, 1971.

Mason, Edward: The Apologetics of Managerialism, *Journal of Business*, Vol. 31, 1958. 1–11.

Mayer, C: Financial Systems and Corporate Investment, *Oxford Review of Economic Policy*, Vol. 3, 1987, 1–16.

———— Financial Systems, Corporate Finance and Economic Development in Hubbard RG (ed.): *Asymmetric Information, Corporate Finance and Investment*, Chicago University Press, Chicago, 1990.

Meade, JE: Is "the new industrial state" inevitable? *Economic Journal*, June, 1968.

McKinsey Emerging Market Investor Opinion Survey 2001 in Corporate Governance: The International Journal of Business in Society Vol. 3, No. 1, 2003.

Menard, Claude (ed.): *Transaction Cost Economics, Recent Developments*, Edward Elgar Publishing Ltd., UK, 1997.

Michie, Jonathan, John Grieve-Smith (eds.): *Globalization, Growth and Governance, Creating an Innovative Economy*, Oxford University Press, Oxford, 1998.

Mills, Geoffrey: *On the Board*, Gower Publishing Co. Ltd., In association with the Institute of Directors, Aldershot, UK, 1981.

Mohanty, Basudev: Slum in Securities Market, Problems and Strategies for Its Sustainable Growth, *Economic and Political Weekly*, October 18–24, Vol. 32, No. 42, 1997.

Monks, Robert AG, Nell Minow: *Corporate Governance*, Blackwell Publishers, Massachusetts, 1995.

———— *Watching the Watchers, Corporate Governance for the Twenty First Century*, Blackwell Publishers, Massachusetts, 1996.

Montgomery, Cynthia: Corporate Diversification, *Journal of Economic Perspectives*, Vol 8, No. 3, Summer 1994, 166.

Montgomery, Cynthia, Rhonda Kaufman: The Board's Missing Link, *Harvard Business Review*, March, 2003.

Mookherjee, Dilip (ed.) *Indian Industry – Policies and Performance*, Oxford University Press, New Delhi, 1997.

Morch, R, Andrei Schleifer, RW Vishny, Management Ownership and Market Valuation – An Empirical Analysis, *Journal of Financial Economics*, Vol. 20, 1988, 293–315.

Mukherjee Reed, Ananya: *Perspectives on the Indian Corporate Economy, Exploring the Paradox of Profits*, Palgrave, New York, 2001.

Murthy, KRS: Corporate Governance: A Sociological Perspective, *The ASCI Journal of Management*, 27 (1 & 2), 1998, 1–9.

Nagaraj, R: India's Capital Market Growth: Trends, Explanations and Evidence,

Economic and Political Weekly, Special Number, September 1996.

Naresh Chandra Committee (August, 2002), Report Published in *Journal of Indian School of Political Economy*, Vol. 14, No. 4, October–December, 2002.

Nayar, Baldev Raj: Business and India's Economic Policy Reforms, *Economic and Political Weekly*, Vol. 33, No. 38, September 19, 1998.

Nickell, Stephen: *The Performance of Companies* (Mitsui Lectures in Economics), Basil Blackwell Inc., Oxford, 1995.

Nigam, Raj K, ND Joshi: *The Pattern of Company Directorships in India*, Research and Statistics Division, Department of Company Law Administration, Ministry of Commerce and Industry, New Delhi, 1963.

Noe, T, MJ Rebello: *The Design of Corporate Boards: Composition, Compensation, Factions and Turnover*, Working Paper, Georgia State University, Atlanta, 1996.

Organisation for Economic Development and Co-operation, *Code on Corporate Governance*, OECD, Paris September, 1999.

Oman, Charles P, Douglas H Brooks, Colin Foy (eds.): *Investing in Asia*, Development Centre, OECD, Paris, 1997.

O'Sullivan, Mary: Sustainable Prosperity Corporate Governance and Innovation in Europe in Michie, Grieve-Smith (eds.): *Globalization, Growth and Governance, Creating an Innovative Economy*, Oxford University Press, Oxford, 1998, op. cit.

Paranjape, HK: *'Socialist' India versus Big Business, A Phoney War*, Manak Paranjape, Pune, 2000.

Patil, RH: Are Institutional Nominee Directors Required? *Economic and Political Weekly*, Review of Industry and Management, Vol. 36, No. 46–47, November 24, 2001, 4380–4384.

Porter, Michael: Capital Disadvantage: America's Failing Capital Investment System, *Harvard Business Review*, September–October 1992, 65–82.

Pound, J: The Efficiency of Shareholder Voting: Evidence from Proxy Contests, *Journal of Financial Economics*, 20, 1998, 237–265.

——— Beyond Takeovers: Politics Comes to Corporate Control, *Harvard Business Review*, March–April 1992, 83–93.

Pozen, Robert C: Institutional Investors: The Reluctant Activists, *Harvard Business Review*, January–February 1994.

Prentice, DD, RPJ Holland (eds.): *Contemporary Issues in Corporate Governance*, Clarendon Press, Oxford, 1993.

PRO NED: *Research into the Role of the NED, London*, 1992.

Prowse, Stephen: *Corporate Governance in an International Perspective*, Economic Paper No. 41, Bank for International Settlements, Basle, July 1994.

RBI: *Report of the Advisory Group on Corporate Governance*, Chairman: RH Patil, March 2001.

Rajiv Gandhi Institute for Contemporary Studies: *Corporate Governance and Ethics, Conference Papers & Proceedings*, RGICS, New Delhi, 1998.

Ram Mohan, TT: Wanted Exit Policy for CEOs, *Economic Times*, September 20, 1999.

Ramu, S Shiva: *Globalization, The Indian Scenario*, Wheeler Publishing, New Delhi, 1996.

Rao, Chalapati KS: Indian Private Corporate Sector: Some Characteristics and Trends, *Company News & Notes*, August 1997.

Rao, Chalapati, MR Murthy, KVR Ranganathan: Some Aspects of the Indian Stock Market in the Post-Liberalization Period, *Journal of Indian School of Political Economy*, Vol. XI, No. 4, October-December 1999, 595–621.

Ray, Rajat K: *Industrialization in India: Growth and Conflict in Private Corporate Sector, 1914–47*, Oxford University Press, New Delhi, 1979.

——— (ed.): *Entrepreneurship and Industry in India, 1800–1947*, Oxford University Press, New Delhi, 1992.

Rechner, PL, DR Dalton, CEO Duality and Organisational Performance: A Longitudinal Analysis Strategic Management Journal, Vol. 12, 1991, 155–60.

Reports on Corporate Governance, Academic Foundation, New Delhi, 2004.

Roe, Mark J: *Strong Managers, Weak Owners: The Political Roots of American Corporate Finance*, University Press, Princeton, 1994.

Romano, Roberta: Corporate Law and Corporate Governance (Chapter 15) in Carrol and Teece (eds.): *Firms, Markets and Hierarchies*, Oxford University Press, Oxford, 1999, op. cit.

Roy, Malay K: *Business Take-Over & the Role of Financial Institutions in India* Academic Foundation, Delhi, 1991.

Rubach, Michael J, Terrence C. Sebora: Comparative Corporate Governance: Competitive Implications of an Emerging Convergence, *Journal of World Business*, Vol. 33, No. 2, Summer 1998.

Rungta, RS: *Rise of Business Corporations in India: 1851–1900*, Cambridge University Press, 1970.

Sarkar, Jayati, Subrata Sarkar: The Governance of India Corporates in Kirit S Parikh (ed.): *India Development Report, 1999–2000*, Oxford University Press, New Delhi, 201–18.

——— *Large Shareholder Activism in Corporate Governance in Developing Countries: Evidence from India*, (Research Monograph), Indira Gandhi Institute of Development Research, Mumbai, October 1999.

Sarkar, Subrata, Anindya Sen: Liberalization of Remuneration Guidelines in India and Its Effect on Managerial Pay: Evidence from Large Corporations, *Vikalp*, Vol. 24, No. 2, April–June, 1999, 35–44.

Sengupta, NK: *Corporate Management in India*, Vikas Publishing House, Delhi, 1974.

——— *Unshackling of Indian Industry, Toward Competitiveness Through Deregulation*, Vision Books, New Delhi, 1992.

Sheridan, TN Kendall: *Corporate Governance, An Action Plan for Profitability and Business Success*, Pitman Publishing, London, 1992.

Shleifer, A, RW Vishny: A Survey of Corporate Governance, *The Journal of Finance*, Vol. LII, No. 2, 1997, 737–783.

Short, Helen, Kevin Keasey: Institutional Shareholders and Corporate Governance in UK, in Keasy, Thomson, Wright (eds.): *Corporate Governance, Economic Management and Financial Issues*, op. cit.

Singh, Ajit: *Take-Overs, Their Relevance to the Stock Market and the Theory of the Firm*, (Monograph), Cambridge University Press, Cambridge, 1971.

———— *Corporate Financial Patterns in Industrializing Economies: A Comparative International Study*, (Technical Paper 2), International Finance Corporation, World Bank, Washington DC, 1995.

———— Financial Liberalization, Stock Markets and Economic Development, *The Economic Journal*, Vol. 107, May 1997, 771–82.

Special Issue on Corporate Governance, *Chartered Secretary*, September, 1998, 927.

Spencer, Anne: *On the Edge of the Organization, the Role of the Outside Director*, John Wiley & Sons, Chichester, 1983.

Smith, Adam: *An Enquiry into the Nature and Causes of the Wealth of Nations*, 1776, Reprinted by JM Dent & Sons, London, 1922.

Stapledon, GP: *Institutional Shareholders and Corporate Governance*, Clarendon Press, Oxford, 1996.

Sudarsanam, PS: *The Essence of Mergers and Acquisitions*, Prentice-Hall India Ltd., New Delhi, 1997.

Summers, C: Codetermination in the United States: A Projection of Problems and Potentials. *Journal of Comparative Corporation Law and Security Regulation* 1982, 155–83.

SEBI Manual, Taxmann Publications, New Delhi, 2001.

Thanjavur: Companies Act Amendment Bill, *Economic and Political Weekly*, Vol. 22. No. 52, December 26, 1987, 2245–49.

The CII Report on Desirable Corporate Governance: A Code, in *Corporate Governance and Ethics*, RGICS, 1998, op. cit.

The King Report on Corporate Governance (South Africa) in *Corporate Governance and Ethics*, RGICS, 1998, op. cit.

Thomas, PJ: *Report on the Regulation of the Stock Market in India*, Government of India, Ministry of Finance, 1948.

Tricker, RI: *Corporate Governance*, Gower Publishing Co. Ltd., Aldershot, England, 1984.

Vives, Xavier (ed.): *Corporate Governance, Theoretical & Empirical Perspectives*, Cambridge University Press, Cambridge, UK, 2000.

Walsh, JP, JK Seward: On the Efficiency of Internal and External Corporate Control Mechanisms, *Academy of Management Review*, Vol. 15, No. 3, 1990.

Ward, Ralph D: *Twenty First Century Corporate Board*, John Wiley & Sons Inc., NY, 1997.

Warther, V: *Board Effectiveness and Board Dissent: A Model of the Board's*

Relationship to Management and Shareholders, Working Paper, USC, 1994.

Watching the Boss: A Survey of Corporate Governance, *The Economist*, January 29, 1994.

Weisbach, Michael: Outside Directors and CEO Turnover, *Journal of Financial Economics*, Vol. 20, No. 1 and 2. 1988.

Weston, J Fred, Kwang S Chung, Juan A Siu: *Take-overs, Restructuring and Corporate Governance*, Prentice-Hall International Inc., New Jersey, 2nd edition, 1998.

Wheeler, David, Maria Sillanpaa: *The Stakeholder Corporation*, Pitman Publishing, London, 1997.

Williamson, OE: *The Economic Institutions of Capitalism, Firms, Markets, Relational Contracting*, The Free Press, New York, 1985.

World Bank, *Corporate Governance: A Framework for Implementation*, 1999. www. worldbank.org/html/fpd/privatesector/cg

Lightning Source UK Ltd.
Milton Keynes UK
25 January 2010

149068UK00001B/28/P